One Sex To The Other:

Reincarnation and the Dual-Gender Soul

By Amy Shapiro, M. Ed.

Published by Amy Shapiro
Gloucester, MA 1930
AmySun@aol.com

This work is dedicated to my spiritual family along with mental health colleagues, and individuals who seek to resolve issues that may have roots deeper than this lifetime.

The Cover: The cover image is a reduction of an original charcoal drawing by the author at age 16 exploring shading and dimension in 1967. It hung privately for 37 years until it came to mind as a visual expression of reincarnating, dual-gender souls.

One Sex To The Other:
Reincarnation and the Dual-Gender Soul

CONTENTS

Chapter One: An Overview Of Past Life Therapy   5
Chapter Two: Confirmations   18
Chapter Three: Scrapping Gender Stereotypes   23
Chapter Four: Three Dual-Gender / Racial Souls   37
Chapter Five: The Need For Love   49
Chapter Six: Paying Karmic Debts   57
Chapter Seven: The Need For Inner Peace   69
Chapter Eight: Healing The Trauma Of Rape   82
Chapter Nine: Friends, Lovers And Betrayal   86
Chapter Ten: Patricide And The Cost Of Hate   90
Chapter Eleven: True Biblical Stories!   95
Chapter Twelve: American History Up-Close   104
Chapter Thirteen: Native American Times   113
Chapter Fourteen: The Fabric Of Community   131
Chapter Fifteen: More Dual-Gender Stories   136
In Closing: The Dual-Gender Legacy   158
Resources   159

INTRODUCTION

Have you ever wondered what it would be like to be the opposite sex? If you have ever imagined it, chances are you were tapping into more than just imagination. You may have been accessing your own unconscious memories from a prior lifetime in which your soul inhabited a body of your opposite sex.

Through past life regression, one may recall having actually lived as the opposite sex, and see that while the soul inhabits a male or female body it is not exclusively male or female. The soul transcends gender stereotypes, beyond limiting cultural standards of beauty, sexual prowess or charisma. By recognizing ourselves as Dual-Gender Souls, we understand that our souls have many goals and aims unrelated to culturally-defined sexual roles or "gender appropriate" behavior as constructs of our social conditioning.

As we consciously review our past lives, we begin to evolve more fully as Dual-Gender Souls, knowing that we are far beyond the limits of social scripts. The past life regression stories in this book are of women and men who discovered at least one prior lifetime in which their souls occupied bodies of the gender opposite to their present life and how both gender identities could then be integrated within the psyche.

These more than forty stories were chosen from hundreds of past life regressions conducted over a span of thirty years of private practice. Each has a dual-gender feature in common, inasmuch as each man reviewed a female past life and each woman reviewed a male past life. These stories express slices of humanity that speak to heart and head, and reveal something about us all by extension.

Some single-gender-soul cases (same-sex past lives) contributed to Chapter One, which discusses the reasons people seek the experience of past life therapy, the dynamics of the regression, the range of soul "purposes" and how insights gained through past life therapy can improve the present. Each dual-gender case begins with why the individual wanted to review his or her past life; their expectations, problems or needs at the time of the session, along with relevant background information. The details of the regression were generated from each person's extrasensory perceptions as seen, heard, felt or sensed from within a state of deep relaxation and expanded awareness during the session. My role as a past life therapist was to guide each person through his/her experience, ask relevant questions and structure the flow of perceptions to maintain coherency.

Once the details of the lifetime are reviewed, each person can see and understand the purpose of that life, the lessons learned, character qualities acquired or the soul obligations fulfilled. These insights are presented in an overview of how the past life relates to the person's present. Each case ends with a brief summary of its therapeutic value to the person.

In terms of my own journey, my belief in reincarnation and quest for spiritual development dates to the 1960s and earlier, as unexplained flashbacks and premonitions taught me that the world is filled with greater mystery than the physical realm reveals. By the time I was 21, I had reviewed dozens of my past lives and began to share my interest and skills with others while completing formal academic and non-academic training. Over the years, I enjoyed encounters with hundreds of people who found healing and peace in reviewing past lives, reinforcing the power of this modality as a therapeutic tool.

As reincarnation steadily grew in popularity, I was delighted by many books on the subject that confirmed that my work was on target. Clients kept prodding me to write MY book about reincarnation but I hesitated, feeling that others already said most of what I might say on the subject. That is, until I realized that a persistent phenomenon in my own practice seemed to be short-changed in other books; the pattern and purpose of souls changing from male to female (or from female to male) bodies as they reincarnate.

I began wondering about the purpose of this trend. Is it just so that we could experience the biological variations of the human race or does our "Dual-Gender Soul" pattern reveal something more important about our development? Once my attention turned to it, dozens of new threads of understanding began to weave into a fabric of compassion, and I knew which "message" was mine to share.

The result is this unusual compilation of stories of healing as a central theme. Chapter One establishes a cultural need to examine and consider the validity of this phenomenon, and continues with an overview of why people explore their past lives, with examples of dual-gender souls. Chapter Two addresses those who struggle to overcome skepticism, sharing dual-gender cases where reincarnation was confirmed through external means. Chapter Three plunges into gender stereotypes that dissolve as we understand our dual-gender soul nature. Chapters Four to Fourteen explore the dual-gender soul idea with stories that demonstrate sub-themes: Dual-Racial Souls, The Need For Love, Paying Karmic Debts, The Need for Inner Peace, Healing the Trauma of Rape, Friends, Lovers and Betrayal, Patricide and the Cost of Hate, True Bible Stories, American History Up Close and Personal, Native American Times, and The Fabric of Community.

Because my clients are mostly women, I invited other Past Life Therapists to contribute Dual-Gender Soul cases of men who recalled female past lives, to better balance male and female cases. Special thanks to those who offered fascinating dual-gender soul stories for Chapter Fifteen: Dr. Bruce Goldberg, Phyllis Nelson Grau, M.A., Rev. Sue Lukegord and Rabbi Yonassan Gershom.

My Closing comments in *The Dual-Gender Legacy* speak of how Dual-Gender Souls have the power to transcend psychosocial stereotypes and prejudices, to live more lovingly and compassionately, where women freely celebrate and manifest their creative drives, and men appreciate and cherish their receptive natures.

Deep gratitude goes to my clients whose urgings prompted this book into being, and whose identities are protected herein. After years of being privileged to hear their rich and varied stories and participate in their healing, it is an honor to share their stories, to encourage and inspire others. Further sincere thanks to Stephen H. Frye, MD, Dean Helen Hickey, Ph.D, Isabel Hickey, Judith Hoffman, M. Ed, Barbara Krieger, Ph.D, Priscilla Mueller, Donna Sabloff, Ph.D. William Swygaard, author of the Awareness Techniques and Sharon Welch, Ph.D. for their valuable input. Boundless thanks to my wonderful family for their support, and particularly my son Clifton for assisting me with formatting, graphics and other vital publishing details.

CHAPTER ONE: AN OVERVIEW OF PAST LIFE
THERAPY – WHY SEARCH?

People seek out the experience of past life regression for many reasons and reincarnation as a belief system is based on a great deal of rational thought. Physics teaches us there is no such thing as a straight line. Space is curved so everything returns. Metaphysically, this principle is known as karma or the cosmic law of cause and effect; what goes around comes around. If you believe that your soul continues beyond this life then logic says you have lived before. Reincarnation is a plausible answer to where you were.

While not everyone needs to explore these dimensions of his or her soul, much can be gained from delving into our past. When we have exhausted all other explanations for problems and conflicts, exploring deeper levels of consciousness can reveal the answers. Such a process in therapy can uncover the source of unconscious blocks that keep us from moving forward through experiences, whether with relationships, work, personality, self-image or dealing with phobias, anxieties or other problems. Past life therapy accesses the roots of problems that are so unconscious, normal psychotherapy simply does not reach them. Going into deeper levels of the psyche, you may find one or more lifetimes where the roots of present problems are based, which can facilitate a tremendous release and healing.

Most people want to see their past lives to answer specific questions, such as: Why was I born in certain circumstances? or "Why am I fascinated with a particular culture or historical period or figure?" Most people have inklings. For example, when you meet someone where you say to yourself, "It feels like I've known him/her before." You want to know where that feeling comes from. People often wonder why one person was born a genius or with a gift in a certain area, and another is not.

Likewise, some people are born into situations that seem quite unjust, perhaps to an alcoholic parent or a dysfunctional family. Perhaps you were orphaned or have had a handicap in your life that has made you wonder, *Is this my only chance at life?* For a child who only lives a few years, is that all there is? Have you ever met someone and intuitively felt you knew that person? Have you ever gone someplace new that looked familiar, where you automatically knew your way around? Perhaps you were there before this life. Reincarnation makes sense in light of these questions.

Have you ever found yourself having an irrational reaction to something and you wondered why it got to you so much? Sometimes, events trigger past life memories within the unconscious mind, reactivating old emotions from unhealed traumas or losses. You may meet souls who were rivals in another lifetime and you feel an instant, irrational distrust or an inexplicable drive to compete with them for power. Souls we knew before come back into our lives to complete old business.

Isabel Hickey, a wonderful spiritual teacher, taught that *love and hate bind us from lifetime to lifetime; if you love anyone enough, you will never lose that person and if you hate anyone enough, that person will never leave you.* That alone is reason enough to source out a relationship from a past life. If you have a problem where you resent someone from the present life, you are wise to complete that relationship so you don't have to meet the person again and work things out in another lifetime. Once you release the anger or hate, you can forgive the person and receive the lesson you needed to learn from that relationship. Even if you were hurt, you become more complete and whole within yourself.

The same is true with love; if you lose someone you love very much, you may meet him or her again in another lifetime. Many people who have lost loved ones want to explore subtler levels of consciousness to reconnect with those loved ones and to reaffirm that they are only temporarily separated. In this way, past life therapy can change your view of death by diminishing the fear of it.

If you see that there is more to life than the years we are here, it dissolves some of the fear of leaving this life. It also doesn't mean you can put anything off, thinking, 'Oh, I'll do it in my next life.' Wrong! If you don't do it now, it can be harder later, so never pass up an opportunity for growth and evolution.

One of the best reasons to explore past lifetimes is to clarify the soul's true present purpose in terms of one's ongoing evolution. Earth is a wonderful school and each incarnation has a unique purpose. We all have things we have to learn and problems to overcome and we choose the circumstances of our births (from a much wiser state of awareness than our normal mentalities) so we can grow and fulfill our spiritual purposes. Perhaps you were born with a talent or gift to share with the world, so you chose parents who would nurture that talent. Many of us have talents from other lives that were not nurtured in childhood and are waiting to be reclaimed. Past life regression can restore these gifts to our conscious awareness.

Past Life Therapy helps to clarify the relationship between body, soul and Spirit. Our Spirits are totally aware of everything we could ever want to know about ourselves. Our souls collect experiences as memory, which goes into a sort of library of records, the *Akashic Records*, where all our soul experiences are stored. To use a computer analogy, your Akashic Records are like a soul microchip. Your soul may be thought of as your psyche or the feeling aspect of your being. Your Spirit is always available to you and never apart from you, even when you separate yourself from it. The soul enters a new body each lifetime and develops a persona with that body but the Spirit transcends the physical.

Speaking of bodies and memories, our etheric bodies carry memory cells from one life to another. If you abuse your own body in one lifetime, the karmic consequence may be to return into a handicapped body in another life. This does not mean a punishing Creator gives us handicapped bodies; our souls know what we need to learn through our life circumstances, so we come into the specific body and unite with the specific set of parents through which we can best learn the lesson.

An often-unintended benefit of past life therapy is greater appreciation for time as a vital aspect of our lives. Once we become aware of the vastness of our souls and what a gift it is to return to Earth to learn, grow and perfect ourselves, we dedicate ourselves with greater passion to realize our potentials and live our present lives to the fullest.

Past life therapy prods us to discover many ways of looking at and experiencing ourselves in time. Seeing past lives involves a kind of simultaneity of time. It really doesn't matter if you categorize the experience as evidence of actually having lived in other times or simply a powerful metaphorical story of what your psyche needs you to process. Through regressing and seeing scenarios that your unconscious brings to the surface, you put your present life into a new perspective.

Most people review past lives for personal reasons rather than for humanitarian purposes, yet the latter is often a by-product, as we discover that we have lived in other countries, cultures and religious faiths, as well as members of the opposite sex, as these stories reveal. Once we understand that others mirror to us the kind of person we once were or may yet become, we can no longer judge each other as being superior or inferior. If each sex were truly to stop judging the other and recognize that we each deserve respect and appreciation for our inherent worth and dignity as dual-gender souls, we would have peace on this planet!

Each of the dual-gender stories in this book begins with the reason why the man or woman wanted to do a past life regression, such as to resolve a problem. The reasons one may seek out this kind of experience vary with each individual. Presenting problems expressed by clients can be grouped into five categories: 1) Relationship karma and/or problems with a specific person, 2) The desire to source out the root of a phobia or talent; 3) The desire to understand the spiritual meaning associated with a life challenge, (such as an illness); 4) The desire to source a feeling connected to a certain historical period or culture; 5) The need for healing.

Experience teaches never to judge the reasons people come for regression. Individuals may state one reason and then reveal more deeply unconscious motivations during the session. All therapeutic relationships begin by building rapport and trust by accepting the client with all his or her fears and worries.

Before concluding a regression session the client is returned to the presenting problem to make sure an opportunity is provided to source out any past life roots associated with that problem. In most cases, relevant unconscious material surfaces to address these problems, allowing the individual to make solid progress toward conflict resolution. Often, conflicts are resolved as a result of past life therapy, which the client may not have realized that s/he had prior to the regression.

The Session: Reviewing Your Soul Records:

Past life regression is a process whereby you review where you were and what you did before this life. Clients in a state of deep relaxation and expanded awareness experienced the details of past lives presented in this book. A term used to describe the viewing of a past life is *running*. Information was generated from the individual's own extra-sensory perceptions in images seen, words heard, emotions or sensations. The role of the past life therapist is to guide clients through their experiences by asking relevant questions to structure the flow of perceptions and to maintain a coherency within the big picture.

Many people wonder if they are in a hypnotic trance state when reviewing these past lives and many hypnotherapists have discovered by chance or design that individuals in trance tap into unconscious memories of past lives. Hypnosis has some similarities to the technique used in these cases, William Swygard's Awareness Techniques. The Awareness Techniques guide individuals to a state of deep relaxation and an expanded state of consciousness.

The Awareness Techniques next guides you to fill your surrounding space or *aura* with light. Once in this state of *integration* you are in communication with your Higher Self or Spirit, which guides you to review the information you need to answer your questions. This information is stored in what mystics refer to as the *Akashic Records*, also known as the 7th Plane of consciousness.

This technique lets you retain full memory of what you see in the session. You are fully conscious in the session of all the information you are processing along with knowing that you are in a room with a guide and can open your eyes at any time if you want to stop the process. You can think of this process as going to a library and reviewing your spiritual archives, visiting that part of your consciousness where the records of past experience are stored. Working with a guide can be useful to help you find the material you need to review.

The Awareness Techniques of regression are easy to learn and most people can learn to do it by themselves. They pose no risk of getting stuck in the past or of creating an altered identity. A logical question to ask is, if we have a number of different past lives, how do we know which one to review? The simple answer is that trust and faith is placed in your own Higher Self or Spirit, which automatically guides you to exactly what you need to see for whatever spiritual work you are doing in the present. If you are working on a relationship and that's the most important thing to you, your Spirit will guided you back automatically to see the past life experience relative to your current relationship situation.

The time required to complete a regression session depends upon the amount of detail an individual runs on any given lifetime. You can spend an hour running one life in detail or you can scan a whole lifetime on an overview basis as if reviewing a synopsis of it. One woman overviewed seven past lives in forty-five minutes, all in answer to a few questions she had about her present.

Another aspect of regression is between-lives awareness. If you review a lifetime four centuries ago, it may be logical to wonder where you were between lives and why you jumped so far back in time rather than reviewing a more recent incarnation. Your own Higher Self or Spirit will show you whatever part of your history is important for your ongoing growth.

We often see in regression what happens between lifetimes after leaving the former body and some of what happens then does relate to the idea of heaven and purgatory. We review our life's experiences on a higher level of awareness; we see what we accomplished and what is still unfinished. We can spend any length of time, or *un-time,* between lifetimes because time is virtually meaningless beyond Earth living. Our Spirits know when we are ready to return to Earth and guide us to reincarnate into the right circumstances for our ongoing evolution.

Related to this is the idea of ghosts or souls that have left the body yet who remain earth-bound. Some earth-bound souls have unfinished work and hover over their former-life circumstances to guard their work until it is finished. Souls with unresolved issues often resist moving on due to attachments to loved ones left behind on Earth who are grieving the departed soul and are keeping that soul from going forward.

We can help Earth-bounds to move on by showing them that they are more than their Earth life and that more wonderful adventures wait for them on the other side, sometimes with souls they know from their lives who left their bodies earlier. Depending upon the circumstances of how someone left the body, s/her may not even realize s/he is dead. This is common if the person was inebriated or drugged at the time of death. S/He may hover over others from that life, wondering why nobody is talking to him/her until it is understood that the former incarnation is over and that it is time to move on to another experience, realm or challenge, perhaps in a new incarnation.

The subject of earth-bounds is separate from past lives, since the person being regressed is obviously incarnate. Yet if someone is causing a deceased loved-one to stay Earth-bound out of selfishness or self-pity, that person needs to let go of the deceased and a regression session can facilitate this release.

Many therapeutic tools are used in the process of conducting an effective past life regression, such as moving forward or backward in time. A good guide can sense when the psychic substance of a review begins to lag, and guide the client to progress to the next significant event in terms of the soul's evolution in that life. A person automatically pauses at important events and describes what is transpiring.

Another important regression tool is distancing oneself from painful emotions associated with the review. This is particularly helpful if the individual reviews a traumatic or violent episode. This is not to advocate repressing emotions, but only that one need not re-subject oneself at close emotional range to past pain that can be viewed and healed at a safer emotional distance. Many clients weep upon seeing the pain, sorrow, losses or sacrifices of past lives. Just as a warm bath comforts the body, tears often unburden the soul of suffering. Crying is a confirming element in regression work because the shedding of tears is evidence that the soul is experiencing something powerfully moving.

Regardless of how eventful or uneventful the details of past lives might seem, it is important that the individual is brought to the very end, to see the circumstances of the death and then go beyond to whatever awaited the soul after that lifetime. Once we see how easily we slip out of our bodies, the fear of death often vanishes, since we know it is not the end but only a release into a brighter, more refined realm of being.

From the vantage of a liberated soul, the individual can understand the purpose of the just-reviewed lifetime, if s/he successfully completed it and how that soul purpose relates to the present. This part of the session helps a person bridge the past life with the present life purpose that remains to be fulfilled, creating a valuable context in which the individual can thereafter hold the regression experience.

These post-lifetime reviews allow the individual to ask Spirit questions about that lifetime or his/her present or future path. This can be very healing and renewing as individuals bathe in the radiant warmth and loving embrace of their own compassionate Spirits. This experience often brings tears of joy stemming from a sense of coming home to a reunion with a spiritual essence so long-desired. That joyful reunion is who they truly are and always will be, in Spirit.

The Purpose of Past Lives:

Much of the therapeutic value of past life regression comes from discovering the soul's purpose in the lifetime that was reviewed. The purpose may be a lesson that needed to be learned, a character trait that needed to be acquired or an obligation that had to be fulfilled. If a past lesson was not fully learned, a way must be found to integrate it into the present life.

Past life regression shows us that we are here to learn the many lessons of this amazing school called Earth. Earth is our souls' laboratory and other people are among our best teachers. On a soul level, the saying that your worst enemy is your best teacher is very true. We learn our most powerful life lessons through our most difficult relationships and a relationship between souls may shift roles from one life to another. Each lifetime tends to have a theme running through it that can be expressed in different ways during the course of a regression. This theme can draw you back to review a specific lifetime to reconnect with it and to restore the unconscious material back into full awareness.

Each of the dual-gender cases in this book includes the purpose of the person's past life as expressed by the individual while in a state of heightened spiritual integration, spoken without regard to grammar or literary style. During this portion of a session, individuals view their lifetimes from the vantage of having just left their former-bodies, looking back before moving on beyond that lifetime. Insights at that stage may relate to high ideals and broad concepts or simple goals and basic tasks in relation to the souls' ongoing evolution. Whatever an individual sees is the purpose of a lifetime is always meaningful and valid for him/her and the purpose of any lifetime is as unique as each individual.

Relative to the present, past life regression can reveal why we chose a particular mate; we may marry people we knew from other lives, not always in the context of friendly relations. Negative experiences also draw us to a particular mate to complete a cycle or balance our karmic books. We may need to forgive ourselves of guilt we have been carrying in our unconscious or we may need to forgive our partners. Love and hate have enormous power in our psyches and they determine which relationships are carried from one life into the next. As our souls evolve, we each do the best we can with what we know at that time. As Isabel Hickey often said, *if we knew better, we would do better.* Past Life Therapy demonstrates that we don't need a separate heaven or hell to reap the consequences of past good deeds or misdeeds. Many hardships we face on Earth are of our soul's own choosing and some individuals regress to see situations where they were very cruel. One woman who came for a regression was timid and shy and seemed afraid of everything. She reviewed a male lifetime as a cruel, vicious pirate who killed many people as sheer sport and loved humiliating and intimidating others who were weaker. In her present life, this woman had suffered terrible neglect by her parents as a girl. All of her teeth were extracted when she was a just a teenager because her parents would not pay for the treatment that could have saved her teeth. She hated her present parents for the suffering they had caused.

When she regressed to see the kind of man she'd been as a pirate, she realized that her soul had chosen her present parents on a higher level of consciousness to compensate for this past.

Strange as it sounds, her soul needed to suffer some of the pain she (as a he) had inflicted on others in order to understand how deeply others had been hurt. Only then could she purge herself of the enormous guilt her soul carried on an unconscious level. She was able to see that by suffering the pain she endured in her present life, she had cleansed herself on a soul level. After reviewing this past life, she was also able to forgive her parents (former victims of the pirate) because she began to have compassion and empathy for them.

When this woman returned for counseling about a year later, she was a different person. She had a wonderful smile on her face (she had not smiled before) and was very happy. She was in love and in a wonderful relationship. She had opened her heart after overwriting the previously unconscious limiting messages of "I'm not worthy; I'm not beautiful; I have no control over my life."

In a single-gender case, a man regressed to see a life as a rogue and ladies man who fathered many children but parented none of them. In his present life, he was afraid of marriage because, as he discovered in regression, he was afraid that the souls of the children whom he fathered but didn't parent in that past life would return as his children in this lifetime to make him miserable. He unconsciously felt unworthy of enjoying a warm, loving relationship with children. Once he faced his past and understood the source of his fears, he communicated his remorse to those souls and inwardly asked for their forgiveness. This was very healing for him and allowed him to embrace the idea of marriage and parenting as an opportunity to atone for his past.

On the subject of past life parent-child relations, one woman told of a time in this life when she was on a mountain climbing trip with her daughter. When she saw her daughter on a cliff admiring the beautiful view, this woman was suddenly struck with a wrenching, horrendous terror. Sweating and hysterical, she grabbed her daughter and pulled her away from the edge, shouting, "Just stay away from that cliff!" Suspecting a deja vu experience, the woman wanted to investigate reincarnation. In her regression, she saw where the soul who was her present daughter met her past-life death off the edge of a cliff. She then understood why that moment had been so terrifying to her. It brought the full trauma of the unresolved emotions from that past life experience into her immediate present.

These flashes and deja vu experiences are probably more common than people might assume, where the memory of a past life trauma remains hidden in the unconscious waiting for a triggering present-life event to raise the emotion up to the surface of the psyche. A fascinating dual-gender example of this was shared with the author in casual conversation in an unlikely setting, a business establishment!

A service representative talking with the author about certain customer options opened up completely upon learning that she was speaking with a past life therapist, and shared a story she had not told to anyone before, yet had haunted her for over twenty years. One night after leaving a party where she had had a great time, she was walking home glowing in the aftermath of the good time. She was just tipsy enough to be a little wobbly as she walked. She was approaching a dangerous intersection where she needed to pay full attention in order to cross the street safely. Suddenly, she experienced herself floating above the pavement and noticed what seemed to be a vivid image of an Irish man whose name she immediately knew, although she her rational mind knew that the man was only in her imagination. She could still picture his facial features and the outfit he wore, in clear detail as she described him. The vision of this man stayed with her only until she got safely across the street, and then disappeared. She had always wondered if she had been seeing herself as she once was in a past life and was delighted to have the chance to ask someone knowledgeable. It was easy to guess that she had indeed been seeing herself as she once was and may have *flashed* on that past life personality at that crucial moment of her former death. The man she had been before was also drunk and was probably knocked out of the body in an accident while in an alcohol-induced state of mind. The triggering even that evoked that image had been the impending danger of crossing a busy street at night while intoxicated. Her soul, having already been yanked out of one body due to past carelessness, did not want to let a second lifetime be similarly cut short.

Past life therapy has been a highly effective treatment method for phobias. When a person sees something that he or she has feared will happen in the future actually did happen in the past, the fear dissolves. When the phobia is gone, the person is free to move on, releasing new creative energy as the old block dissolves.

In one phobic case, a man was afraid to have anything around his neck and was troubled by this phobia because he led an extremely public life as a media celebrity and often attended gatherings that required wearing a tie. He believed in the power of mind over matter, so he was baffled by his inability to control this seemingly irrational fear. He reviewed a past life where he was hung for a crime he hadn't committed. He had unconsciously implanted this memory-cell as a type of fear in the neck region of his etheric body (the energy field which emanates some inches beyond the physical limits of a person's body). This fear was reactivated whenever his neck was touched. After this past life regression, he was able to wear a tie snugly tied without any anxiety.

Each dual-gender story presented in this book is discussed in relation to the individual's present life as stated in the person's own words and as a therapeutic summary. Special attention is given to the way new doors of perception opened to the person as a result of reviewing a life lived in the body of the opposite sex. Hopefully these stories will inspire readers to expand their own dual-gender perceptions of personal possibilities.

CHAPTER TWO: CONFIRMATIONS

Sometimes, we are able to confirm the validity of our existence in past lifetimes through concrete evidence. The following four Dual-Gender stories are examples of confirmations. Only the last story was preserved in note form at the actual time of the session, and so contains actual client quotes. The others are drawn from my own vivid recollections of the regression sessions.

Partners Again

In the early years of exploring the Awareness Techniques, I was fortunate to develop a close friendship with a young woman who became a personal partner to me in exploring these realms. For nine months, we took turns running each other (guiding each other in the Awareness Techniques process) to familiarize ourselves with where we had been in other lifetimes. During one session, I reviewed a male past life as a Russian mountain climber who was tall and rugged. I reviewed all the significant details of the lifetime and then we took a break. When I ran my friend, she seemed to be reviewing the same lifetime as I had just reviewed! When she came down to her first view of her past lifetime, she said, "Gee, I'm so-and-so's wife." I thought to myself, "Oh, this is very interesting" and asked her to tell me all about it. She recounted the lifetime as she saw it.

And then I thought, "Well here's my opportunity to confirm if this was a valid technique." I had not described three specific things, my appearance, my wife's appearance and our home, all of which I had seen. When I asked her to describe her own and her husband's appearance, and their house, she described each exactly as I had seen them.

I was glad to learn that our friendship had roots in other lives and that our soul connection was very deep. That session took place during the early 1970's, when the seeds of feminism were taking root in our culture and women were becoming more vocal about expressing their chagrin at their second-class status. Discovering a male past-life identity within me put many things in a new perspective that included and went beyond feminism.

Verified in the Library

In another confirmation of reincarnation, a woman regressed to a lifetime as an American Indian, and saw where she was and the name of the tribe. She saw how the leader of their tribe was killed, after which the whole tribe fell apart. She, as a male Indian, was really angry and carried a tremendous amount of rage. Yet, if you met this woman today, you would think she couldn't harm a fly. But in her regression, she was furious and wanted to kill lots of people, but didn't. Seeing this helped put her own anger issues into a better perspective.

Months after her regression, she went to a library and found a book on that particular Indian tribe, which she had never studied in school. She found a reference to the exact tribe to which she belonged, located just where she had seen it during her regression. The story she had seen was as an important part of Native American history, where the chieftain was murdered and the tribe had fallen apart for many years after. The tribal chief's name was written in the book exactly as she had heard it in the regression.

Once a Killer, Now her Husband

A woman who was unhappy in her marriage and also had a lot of other problems regressed back to a lifetime where she was a six-year-old boy whose parents had just left their apartment to do a few errands. A robber broke into the apartment, not expecting to see the little boy. He panicked and killed the boy so the boy couldn't be a witness to the robbery.

During her regression, this woman saw that in her present lifetime she married the same soul whom, as a complete stranger, had broken into the apartment and killed her/him as a boy. On a soul level, she was driven by tremendous hatred for this man who had hurt her and robbed that boy of his life. She married the man who was that same soul in this lifetime — not out of love, but out of revenge, and she hurt him very much in this lifetime. No wonder she was stuck in an unhappy marriage!

Unconsciously, she was holding onto the relationship, wanting to hurt him. Consciously, she didn't know why she was unhappy and making him miserable. Seeing this was very healing for her as she was able to forgive this man's soul and resolve other problems that stemmed from that lifetime, too, involving her parents.

One might expect the robber would repeat the pattern and try to kill her again, but when you leave an incarnation, you review the life on a soul level, looking back to judge it for yourself. When this man looked back and judged what he'd done, he had great regrets. He saw that what he did was wrong and felt the need to make up for it to relieve his soul of the guilt. So he came into his present lifetime with a deep sense of obligation and a desire to rectify things. He found the same soul who was now a woman and devoted his life to making her comfortable, giving her everything she wanted and serving her every need. He married her out of a sense of obligation, wanting to balance his records with her through serving her. On more than one occasion, he called me in desperation, saying, "I can't do enough for her. I can't reach her. I don't know what it is." He was bending over backwards to please her and provide for her.

To all appearances, he was a model husband. But none of us can know why two people are together without knowing the past life connections that are not apparent on the surface. She, on a soul level, knew that he had taken her out of the body at a young age. Her soul had harbored enormous anger towards him and married him out of revenge, to make his life miserable and to make him pay for a past neither consciously remembered.

Now, here is the most amazing part of this story: once she forgave him on a soul level, she exclaimed, "Oh, my God, my back doesn't hurt anymore!" I asked what she meant, as I had not known that she had a back problem. She said, "I've had a chronic pain in my back and it's completely gone now!" When I asked how long she'd lived with this pain, and when she first noticed having a pain in her back, she gasped and said, "Ever since I first met my husband!"

The pain, which healed itself the moment she forgave him, was at the very spot in her back where he had stabbed the little boy in that lifetime. She had carried these memory cells in her etheric body ever since that murder. Meeting him triggered the unconscious memory of that stabbing pain in her back, which she carried for years until she understood it and forgave him. Along with her bitterness, her pain dissolved.

This particular case also demonstrates that there are reasons we choose to reincarnate through our present parents. Imagine the past-life parents' shock and trauma when they returned to find the gruesome scene. They must have suffered terribly the rest of their lives. During her regression, my client saw that she incarnated to the same parents as before. Understandably, they had over-protected her this time to the extreme. Their unconscious fears of harm coming to her, stemming from that past lifetime drove them to suffocate her with excessive attention, to the point where she experienced little of life before she married. Ironically, her primary (conscious) reason for marrying this man at a young age was to escape her parents' unbearable grip! Seeing the whole story prepared her to forgive her parents, too, for having overprotected her in this lifetime. It made perfect sense! Seeing how past patterns relate to the present paves the way for cognitive understanding and empathy. That is the point at which the guide or past life therapist can most effectively ask the person, *"Are you ready to forgive (Name)?"* Usually they are. The moment of true forgiveness releases a watershed of energetic healing, the long-term impact of which does immeasurable good.

Remembering the Dungeon

Once, while conducting a Past Life Therapy Workshop at a local college adult education program, a woman told a fascinating story that held our group spellbound, confirming the reality of reincarnation again beyond imagination. She had been to England as a small child with her family. When they were going through a royal palace there, she said to the tour guide, "I want to see the dungeon downstairs." He said, oh, there's no dungeon downstairs, and she insisted, "Yes there is!" After she described it in detail, he looked at her and paled, saying, "Wow, now that I think of it, there is that dungeon downstairs, but it's not part of the tour. It's been closed off to the public for years and years."

When she was guided in a regression years later as an adult, she saw that she had lived in that building as a man in another lifetime and had many experiences going in and around that very dungeon. When she was a tiny child with her parents visiting that castle in the present life, there was no way of explaining how she knew what was downstairs, except to assume that she was somehow very psychically gifted. What she had experienced as a child was true deja vu, which is far more common in children than most adults might think. Children have fewer personality layers veiling or screening out the wisdom and intuitions of their souls.

CHAPTER THREE:
SCRAPPING GENDER STEREOTYPES

In many respects, all the dual-gender stories presented in this book fit the title of this chapter, as they encourage us to dissolve stereotypical thinking. Yet, the stories in this chapter punctuated the message for five clients whose perspectives about gender stereotypes were greatly altered as a result of their past life regressions.

Inner Strength

Men too often feel trapped by macho stereotypes that they learned to develop throughout their growing years. While some men may find the image of a rugged persona to be a fine role model, other men may experience that image as an obstacle to both their own emotional growth, and to enjoying meaningful relationships with women.

Steve was struggling to reconcile the idea that *real men* dominate women with his conflicting emotional attraction for assertive women. The stereotype of the strong, powerful male had been deeply reinforced through generations of Italian males within his family. At the time of his regression, Steve was a 36-year-old bachelor who felt that this conflict was keeping him from being able to commit to a stable relationship. He felt captivated by a very take-charge woman, yet intimidated by her strong will and personality, and confused about the feelings she stirred in him.

Steve had nurtured an interest in meditation and spirituality over many years and was open to the possibility that he had lived before. He wondered if he and his girlfriend had known each other in a past life, and if that might help him understand his dilemma. His familiarity with meditation along with his earnest desire to solve this riddle made Steve a good candidate for regression.

Steve regressed to the year 1516, to a past life as a seventeen-year-old female named Joan. Joan was wearing black shoes with a square buckle and a brown dress, in a small English village. She was waiting for a man to arrive in whom she was interested. The man was *"a real strong person."* After a few years, they married, making a home where she felt *"comfortable and protected."* Their house was *"basic but warm, made of wood, with a big fire place."*

Moving ahead to the next important event of that lifetime, Steve saw that Joan's husband had become incapacitated due to a serious accident he had while working with wood. The accident resulted in the loss of one of his arms and, understandably, his morale. Thereafter, Joan's husband was *"not himself"* as he could no longer work as before and he assumed that Joan would feel that he was now less of a man. To his great relief, his fears were unfounded. Joan did not think less of her husband as a man; indeed, her love for her husband grew.

For the first time in their relationship, Joan became a source of strength for her husband and found great joy in this new role, knowing her husband could rely now upon her. Their commitment to each other pulled them through very difficult times. The couple was childless, but stayed together, drawing strength from each other's presence until the end of their lives. Joan died first, in her 50's. From the vantage of being outside the body after her death, Steve saw Joan's husband sitting at a table, wearing a beard. Steve recalled the purpose of that life:

> It was a mutual endeavor; I was learning about mutual dependency. The lost arm forced us to find another way of getting strength and to have confidence that another person can be there.

As a result of his regression, Steve understood that strength and endurance are not the exclusive qualities of men, as he was raised to believe, but are just as natural for women. This insight allowed him to go beyond his previous unbalanced *macho* persona that prevented him from experiencing real intimacy in relationships with women. By regressing to a female past life, he saw that superficial gender stereotyping had kept him from feeling truly whole in himself and from seeing women as whole beings. He no longer felt threatened by strong women and no longer needed to repress his feelings of vulnerability, which he had previously viewed as strictly feminine qualities.

Not long after that session, Steve entered a more loving, committed relationship, which led to a lasting and fulfilling marriage of many years. The woman had a daughter by her first marriage. Steve became a devoted parent to the girl and did not let his former gender stereotypes interfere with his ability to love and guide the child. Seeing himself as once having been a strong and compassionate woman freed Steve to more completely love a wife, a daughter and himself.

Obesity and the Weight of Power

Sue Ann needed to uncover the source of her problem. At the time of her session, Sue Ann was unhappy with her appearance and complained of having a hard time managing her weight. This was an obstacle to her feeling fulfilled in love, as her poor self-image got in the way of nurturing healthy relationships with men. She wondered if something from a past life might be related to her body image, especially as it pertained to being overweight.

Sue Ann's Spirit guided her to the exact portion of her soul records that held the key to understanding her dilemma. Sue Ann regressed to see herself as a thirty-five year old male cleric named Charles, in England sometime around 1695. He was wearing black shoes with high lacing and pointy toes, and long, dark, flowing clothes that came down to the floor. She described the imagery of that lifetime in vivid detail:

> I'm in a cold, huge castle, with thick walls, long corridors and big rooms. I'm doing something. I'm very big. I have

a huge, smooth, round belly, not flabby, just big. My stomach always leads when I walk. I feel tired that I have to carry all this weight around. ... I'm a Bishop, and weight signifies power and authority. I'm supposed to be leading these people, as a spiritual leader, but I didn't feel like the position was spiritual. There was so much decision-making. I didn't feel like it was really my responsibility to make decisions about people's spiritual lives, but that was what the church wanted me to do, although I was uncomfortable with it.

Sue Ann regressed further back to review Charles' childhood and see how he knew he would become a member of the clergy:

I was my parents' first born. It was the rule, to bring the family great honor. I was groomed for it. I led an inactive life, wasn't allowed to do a lot of physical activity that other kids my age were doing. I began to put on weight from eating and studying. At first, I wasn't happy. Later, as I got heavier, I justified intellectual pursuits and learned to like that.

Although Charles had been groomed for a religious life, he also had personal desires. Sue Ann saw that Charles had known love in his life:

There was a young girl my age. She was being tutored by the same tutor as I had. I liked her, but we were kept separated as soon as it was recognized that there was mutual interest. My mother loved me. It was a detached love. She knew I had a different destiny.

I had one sister, about six years younger. She seemed very delicate. My parents worried about her. I wasn't too interested.

When Sue Ann progressed forward to view the end that life, she saw that things ended badly for Charles:

> I was 49. There was an insurrection. People were unhappy... there didn't seem to be enough food or money or clothing for them. They were very angry with those of us in the castle with an overabundance of what we needed. I tried to get food and clothing to them, but it was a last ditch effort. They were attacking us, so we fled. I was attacked by a band of peasants who killed us. It was very savage; they stabbed me with swords and mutilated the body.

Once out of the body, Sue Ann summarized the purpose of that lifetime and how it relates to her present, especially as it concerns her body image:

> To use authority more benevolently, not to have conformed to the dictates of an absent church... I am an authority of what I know. I just need to own it for myself, in order to be comfortable taking on leadership roles in my life. My sister then is my oldest daughter now. This time I can be present to her. I can express love and be without reprisal, to have a warm, loving relationship with her, and she can accept it.

> My negative body image is one of the things I can be free from now; I know now it's okay to be intellectual and also physically active. That was where people were getting caught up, using weight as authority, assuming positions of respect out of their heaviness.

Before closing the session, I guided Sue Ann in a creative visualization exercise, whereby she imagined her physical body looking the way she wanted, investing that image with desire. By understanding what was previously an unconscious conflict between her desire to use her intelligence and her fear of being overweight, (which had made Charles a target of anger and revile in the past), Sue Ann was free to be active both physically and intellectually.

This regression brought to light another unconscious issue, which played a role in Sue Ann's self-image. The weight of obedience to an absent church had forced Charles, as a Bishop, to act in a way that betrayed his conscience and the people he was supposed to be serving. Sue Ann can now celebrate being free to follow her own conscience, true to herself, without worrying about retribution from any outside authority. Recognizing a connection between Charles' life as a celibate Bishop and her present shyness about intimacy and commitment was also helpful for Sue Ann.

The dual-gender nature of this regression session helped Sue Ann see that men who hold positions of power can be just as unhappy as women who don't have the privileges and burdens of power. This understanding gave her a new perspective about men, which could foster more fulfilling future relationships. No longer would she need to be intimidated by powerful men, nor resent their authority, knowing how illusory it really is. Now if Sue Ann wants to *"throw her weight around,"* she knows she doesn't have to do it from inside an overweight body!

A Healthy Roar

Suppose for a moment that your emotions were capable of emitting sound-vibrations in your psyche, with each emotion being its own instrument. Imagine the sound of peace or depression or joy. No doubt, some sounds of emotions would be more pleasant to hear than would others. The voice of Lisa's emotions had become too strong for her to ignore, much as she tried. Lisa reported feeling a *"roaring"* energy inside of her and feared that if she *"let it out"* she might *"do something amoral"* she later would regret. The internal tension this created was paralyzing Lisa to the point of fearing the consequences of every natural impulse. Her fear seemed connected to a general anxiety over loss of control, and she wondered if it might have past life roots. She regressed to see herself as a thirty-six year old man in Austria in the year 1840. He was wearing big, clown shoes, purple silk pants, a red silky shirt and make-up:

> I'm on a street with bright colored stores. I'm looking around. There's a feeling of sadness and confusion.

Lisa went back further in time to see what caused this feeling, and continued to review how that life developed:

> Something about a baby, but I don't know. There's a man where I live who seems very violent. He has a sword and he has been violent to me. He is my father. There's a woman there, my father's friend. She seems very bitchy. We're outside and somebody's holding the baby and everybody's fighting. The baby's mother is holding it. She's my mother. I'm not sure what they're fighting about. When it's over, I feel dejected...

Lisa jumped ahead in time to the next significant events, at ages 14 then 18:

> I've been trained to put soles on boots. I work with a cobbler until I'm 18. At age 18, I'm riding on a horse, trying to notify somebody on horseback about some commotion, about somebody who came in a red shirt. I'm a lot stronger for some reason. I now have a more positive image about myself... A few years pass. I see a bird fly off of my arm. It's a message that I don't need to hide. It had to do with being more forceful and stronger... At 22, I was happy. There was a woman I liked then, and she liked me too. When I was 24, a baby girl was born to this woman and myself. I feel very happy. I support my family with

the boots again. I'm content with it. It doesn't matter so much.

The next significant development occurred at age 36:

> Again, there's a feeling of sadness and I see that clown. The little girl and I are crying. I don't see the mother. She died when the girl was real little. It's difficult to manage without her. I've been cooking.

Moving to the end of that lifetime, Lisa saw:

> I live to be 84, but at the end I don't feel like I'm done yet. I like who I am and don't plan to leave.

Clowning around was a good defense mechanism for coping with the profound loss of his wife's death, hiding tears behind smiles for the sake of his daughter. Lisa discovered that the purpose of that lifetime and its relationship to her present life concerned energy and love. She even discovered a kindred dual-gender soul in her present family circle:

> My soul's purpose was to learn that energy is freedom. It feels like the energy isn't confined to this particular person. My current brother was my wife in that life. We're very close, and he feels very connected to my children. He takes great interest in them.

During her post-review time, while still integrated with her Spirit-consciousness, Lisa asked how to best use her enhanced energy:

> A purple window is opening up and energy flies through it. I need the attitude that this energy is my friend.

Lisa realized that she had been living in fear of the man her former father had been, who had misused power and energy. She saw similar connections with her present father, who loomed large in her consciousness and toward whom she felt an enormous amount of repressed anger. The energy she had consumed by repressing this anger was the roaring feeling that she needed to release. Once Lisa accepted her anger as healthy and not necessitating out-of-control behavior, she began to recover her true life force. During a guided creative visualization process, she said about her father:

> I'm making him littler and littler. I feel my heart opening up and he gets out. I've released him and forgiven him. There's a light of loving energy coming in now.

Like other women, Lisa had been conditioned to believe that anger is unbecoming to a girl, but she was now ready to override that stereotype, to reclaim the justifiable, healthy roar of a person unfairly treated or abused. Just as Lisa had learned to embrace her nurturing and protective instincts when she was a man and widower in her past life, she could now begin to achieve a greater sense of wholeness by embracing her drive for self-empowerment.

The Trappers Wife, Biker's Lover, now her Mother

Whether or not we ever act publicly in a theatrical play, we may feel various characters bubbling up inside of us at different times, each seeking expression. These feelings may be veiled memories of past incarnations representing different sides of our natures. That is what Fran discovered through her past life regression, as well as a special dual-gender bond with her mother and the inner peace she desired.

Fran had been practicing meditation for many years and was ready to explore deeper levels of awareness. She hoped a past life regression would give her new spiritual direction. Of the three lifetimes Fran reviewed in our session, two were as males. One was a Trapper and the other was as a Free Spirit.

Trapper

In the first male lifetime that Fran reviewed, she lived somewhere in the United States in the mid-1800s, as a twelve-year-old boy named Allan, wearing a brown shirt, jeans and belt:

I'm walking in the woods from a village. I'm hunting. I have a knife. I'm hunting rabbits.

Fran moved forward in time within that life to review how things developed:

I've gotten married. I'm between 35 and 40 years old. My wife is younger, kind of pretty, with long hair. We have two kids, a girl and a boy. I want to take care of them and make sure they're warm and fed. I have a small log cabin house. We're happy and fed. We live out away from the community in the woods. We met in a square dance. I was age 25 or so. When we first met, she was pretty and I felt warm. I was a trapper. When I'm trapping, I walk the river and I trap fox. I have a gun. I walk the woods and spend the whole day walking and checking on the traps. I take its leg and throw it on my back, take it home, skin it and use the meat. The skins are used. I tack them on wood in the barn and dry them. When they're dry I load 'em up on a cart and take 'em into town and sell 'em at the store. Then I come back with food.

It's 1853. My kids are getting older and having their own families. I'm alone with my wife. I see the two of us sitting together and I'm smoking a pipe, rocking in a chair... I'm 73 years old. I'm lying on the bed with a quilt on me. I'm alone. I've been sick. My wife's dead.

Fran's past life purpose was fairly simple yet very meaningful to her in relation to her present:

> The relationship to the family, that I'm capable of having one... My wife then is my current mother.

Moving beyond that incarnation, Fran reviewed a female lifetime followed by another male lifetime. The female life was short and painful: she was crippled as a girl due to a horse-and-carriage accident, then lonely and neglected by her family until she died in her late teens. Given her physical limitations and the abandonment she suffered, Fran greatly enjoyed reviewing her next life as a daredevil, free-spirited man:

Free Spirit

Fran was a large 37-year-old man on a motorcycle in 1927, in the mid-west:

> I'm driving very fast, I fall off, and the motorcycle falls. I get rid of the motorcycle. I get up and walk away, and feel free for some reason. It was like an awakening. I travel a lot. I'm single. I feel really, really happy. I do odd jobs, work in kitchens. I work in this one little diner. I really like it there, the people. I meet a waitress there. It's my present mother again. We're really happy. ... I leave. I don't stay. I'm free-spirited. I don't want to settle down. I go west. I'm walking, still real happy. I go to Arizona, see a lot of cactus. I go to some kind of a commune. It's a real flat little house. I stay there and work in the kitchen. That's where I learn to meditate...

> At the end, I'm about 50 years old. Something hits me on the tip of my head again, a big rock off a ledge. I fall down, down in a canyon. I'm just there, alone.

As before, Fran saw the purpose of that life and its relationship to her present:

> To learn inner peace; I need to expand on this peace. Other people don't understand the free-spirited side. It's okay to be alone and not to fight it so much.

These male incarnations showed Fran two sides of her own nature; one devoted to family and the tasks of daily survival that keep a family together, and another side that is free-spirited and content to be alone. Fran felt a greater sense of permission about being alone, that it was equally okay for a woman to be alone as for a man. The inner peace she felt in both lives is the peace she desired again, more than a relationship or job.

Curiously, the soul of her current present mother was a love tie in both male lives. Coming into her present life as a daughter to the same soul she twice loved as a man allowed them to be close again, now as women. Fran was a very receptive student to learning everything she needed to know about feminine ways from her mother.

As a healthy young woman able to care for herself, Fran did not wish to limit her options by committing prematurely to the responsibilities of family life. Fran accepted the simple spiritual guidance that she could be at peace while also being alone, a truth that many women are conditioned to deny, causing anxiety and insecurity in our culture. It was this meaning of *free-spirited* to which Fran referred when she said, *"most people don't understand the free-spirited side".*

A Vegetarian-Divorcee's Dilemma

Barbara was a new divorcee and single mother raising two sons. She was afraid that her anger at her ex-husband's infidelities would sour her ability to raise her sons, toward whom she did not want to misdirect her bitterness toward their father.

Barbara was in the process of making several decisions about their future and hoped that a regression session could give her better perspective on her choices. One of her decisions involved food, as she was a vegetarian and unsure as to whether she should raise her sons to be vegetarians, too.

Barbara seemed unfazed at finding herself in the body of a man. In fact, she reviewed more than one lifetime as a man, but only one in substantial detail. In that male life, she regressed back to the year 1627, to the forest of what is now New York. His name was Torontasaw and he was thirty- five years old, wearing beaded moccasins with fringe, fur tails and one thick braid. From the perspective of Torontasaw's eyes, Barbara described his community and lifestyle:

> There are small animals. I'm living with a group of people who fish and hunt small animals for food. I'm unhappy about killing. Nature is good and powerful. There are lots of kids and a lot of responsibilities. I see two women who could be wives. I'm a good provider. There's no question about what is required of each of us; we understand and do what we must do. There's a lot of happiness and no jealousy. But there is a problem with too many kids; there is never enough food.

Barbara continued to review that lifetime, which went along rather uneventfully. By the end, Torontasaw had quite a crop of offspring to surround him:

> I get to be really old, white haired, cranky, tired and ready to lie down. I outlive my wives. My children take care of me. There are lots of kids and grandchildren now.

Barbara saw the purpose of that lifetime and how it relates to her present life. The message was simple and clear:

Responsibility... Eating was a conflict, which is why I became a vegetarian. I see now, it's not necessary to worry, as long as what is eaten is offered up in fall consciousness. Also, gentleness... I was harsh with the little kids because they never had enough but there was a lot of sharing. There's always enough.

Barbara scanned two more male lives that she casually called, *"stud lifetimes; I recharged the batteries of the females."* Seeing that she wasn't a monogamous man made Barbara feel better about her ex-husband and men in general. It would be hard for her to pass judgment on behavior that, as a former man, she found acceptable. While Barbara neither condones nor emulates promiscuity, she is also no longer as angry about her ex's shortcomings. Her regression also gave her confidence as the primary parent of her sons, since her present obligations paled in comparison to how many children's mouths required feeding in the forest. She was more grateful now than ever to have only two!

CHAPTER FOUR:
THREE DUAL-GENDER / DUAL-RACIAL SOULS

The following stories of individuals who reviewed past lives that revealed dual-gender/dual- racial legacies urge us to reflect on our attitudes toward not only the opposite sex, but toward different races. They show that our souls may choose to incarnate as different racial identities and that doing so fosters deeper respect, tolerance and compassion for all races over time. In addition to these cases, three more dual-racial stories are presented in Chapter 13, Native American Times.

From Black to White

Women accept stereotypes and generalizations about men just as often as men do about women. Two such generalizations are that men have the material advantage in any given situation and that they always choose or control their circumstances. Through her past life regression Marilyn found out how wrong those stereotypes about men can be.

Marilyn was in the process of a divorce at the time of her session and although she did not regret the impending divorce, she was anxious about the radical changes in lifestyle it meant, including a major change of residence. She hoped to find something in a former life that might boost her confidence to handle her current transitional period.

Marilyn saw a time when she was a 'he' who endured far more difficulty than posed by any of her present challenges. She regressed to see herself as a barefoot, young black man in his 20's named Harry, in 1834, wearing pants and a white shirt, in the ocean off the island of Trinidad:

I'm on a sailing ship. It's impressive. I'm close enough to see the shape of the sails. It's moving at a fast clip. There's something I long to do, but I can't. I'm alone.

Moving ahead in time until the boat Harry was on reached its destination, then running the lifetime forward, Marilyn reviewed these details of Harry's life:

> There's a shack with a straw, thatched roof. I have a menial job on a sugar plantation, or a rubber plantation. There's an important man - white — an authority. I go to him. He gives me advice. I'm respectful and I follow it as well as can be expected. There's a woman who becomes my wife later. Right now she's a friend.

Progressing further, Marilyn viewed a sad ending, with no mention of what happened to Harry's wife:

> I'm 54 and longing for things I couldn't do because of my race. I die a natural death.

The purpose of this lifetime in terms of Marilyn's soul evolution was given in the broken English that Harry would have used:

> Accepting my fate. A lot of frustration. It's hard not to be bitter. It's important to know that the feelings were okay and that things would even out. White man was a real friend.

Although there didn't seem to be many clear parallels between that life and Marilyn's present life, some links did exist. When asked how that lifetime related to her present, Marilyn said:

> Being alone or separate was an issue then and I vacillate now between wanting to be a part of things and going my own way. I was safe and cared for then, just as through my marriage, but I wasn't allowed to really grow they way I would have liked. The conflict was, and is, between my need for acceptance and the need to be who I'm becoming.

Harry had survived difficulties in the past while being at a social and cultural disadvantage. This echoed her fears of being disadvantaged in the present. As in the past, Marilyn now needed to risk trusting others; in that life, the limits of Harry's social circumstances dictated what he could do. Now Marilyn was ready to manage her own life and 'even things out'. Through Marilyn's dual-gender experience, she saw that being a man doesn't guarantee wealth, power or social status, and this insight kept her from becoming bitter toward men in general.

From White to Black

Miranda was young to be exploring reincarnation but was a self-confident, mature 22-year-old African-American who was completing her BA degree and wanted to be a doctor. She wondered if she had known any of her female friends in past lives and if her relationship with Will, a married man with whom she was in love, was rooted in a past life. Will loved Miranda but was married. Miranda would not engage in an illicit affair and was struggling to move on emotionally. She hoped that a regression would shed some light on this attachment. She reviewed a past life as a 32 year-old Caucasian man in Spain in the mid 1400s:

> I'm wearing black boots with gold buckles, white stockings all the way up to the thigh, short billowy pants, a green vest closed over a shirt with ruffles. My name is Carlos. I'm holding a tomato in a market place, thinking about how much it costs. The price is okay so I buy the tomato to eat on my way home. A lot of people are around one of the stands. Smoke is coming from that stand and an old woman is there, smoking some kind of meat. She's kind of shabby. I'm walking by a river now. There are long thin boats similar to canoes; they don't seat a lot of people. I stop on the bridge and yell down to a man I know.

He's selling something. I'm just teasing him and he teases me back. I have a happy disposition; I'm kind of skipping along. I'm at home; it's not really a big house. It's a rectangular building. We live in the bottom part. There's a loft upstairs. My sister sees me and smiles. She is knitting with a machine. My mother is kind of large. She's sitting at a table counting money. My father is a carpenter. He's at work. He's a thin man, only about fifty years old. He's friendly; there are no tensions between us. We have a stove with brick walls. As you enter the door on the far right, there is a long bench with a table in front of it. My father built the furniture. I didn't want to learn carpentry skills but my father's okay with that because I do something better; I'm a doorman for a man who is associated with royalty. I stand very still at the door of his castle, just watching. I'm around a bunch of girls in their late teens, early twenties. There are ten or twelve of them, just kind of running around. I announce someone's presence when they come in.

The girls are friends. One girl is the reason for my happy disposition. She has a long neck, light brown hair, blue eyes, wearing a pink dress. We don't have a personal relationship. My other duties are to bring things to the kitchen. My employer is close to a royal family or king. He inspects me and makes sure I'm ok.

At age 18, I got to dance with her, hold her hand and we talk a little bit. When she sees me she giggles. At age 21, my father burns his arm a fire but he doesn't die. He was trying to control a fire in the fireplace. He can't work after that and he's sick. He's open to infection. My mother bakes breads and my sister weaves. I still work at the castle. At age 22, my mother is pressuring me to get married. I still have my eyes on the girl in the castle but I know it can't work. She has a suitor. She hangs around where I work a lot. Her suitor comes with her but she's courteous in front of me. At age 23, I meet a nice girl named Viola. She's skinny with long dark hair and brown eyes. She's of my same class and has a charming disposition. She's quiet and docile and sells flowers with her mother. We met when I bought a flower for the girl in the pink dress. By age 24, we're married and we have a son. I become kind of a supervisor at the castle, looking over the boys at the door. I still see the girl from time to time. She married that suitor. I love her but I accept that it's not meant to be.

I die of a fever at age 37 one week after saving someone from drowning in the river, a girl who was selling something in a boat. It tipped over and she couldn't swim. I jumped from the bridge. I injured myself when I jumped into the water, an internal injury on my left side. My family watched me die, unable to do anything to save me. We had three children by then, a boy and two girls. I'm outside of the body now, floating. I can see my mother, sister, children and wife over the bed where I am. I feel grateful toward them. I'm not joyous or sad, just calm.

The purpose of that lifetime was about freedom, of expression and occupation. In that life, I was free to do something different from my father. That lifetime was a long, long time ago, one of my first lifetimes of freedom. Being male, Carlos had it easier. As a woman now, I have to fight other people's thoughts about me, especially as a black woman.

I chose a woman's body this time because I had experienced being a man again even before that lifetime and I had to understand that things aren't always so easy as they were in my lives as a white male. In those lives I was just in my place, but I had money and work. I was in a low class but still had a royal position and a lot of dignity in my lifestyle. This time, I am supposed to really understand and express love in all aspects and to share that understanding with others.

Miranda saw that the boy in the boat to whom Carlos had yelled in a friendly way from the bridge was one of her current friends. The upper class girl Carlos loved is now Will. Miranda and Will are now free to express their feelings, but another marriage is in the way again. Miranda saw that this was progress, however small, and that they may yet be together, if not in this life then in another. Miranda briefly saw an earlier life as a young man who was stabbed in a fight over a girl, and died as a result of inadequate medical attention. The early deaths in these lives put Miranda's career aspirations into a new perspective, since, had medical care been available in those past lives, those young deaths could have been avoided. No one had urged Miranda to pursue a medical profession, yet she was convinced that it was what she should do, and she now better understood her motivation to become a doctor despite the absence of social pressure for her to do so. Having seen two past lives as men for whom things had come easily, Miranda was determined to achieve her present goals and was ready to commit the time and effort required to overcome all barriers to success, might they be gender- or racial-based.

From Asian to Caucasian

Investigating past lives often impacts one's perception of what might become of him/herself and of loved ones after their present lives. That was Paula's greatest wish and intention in seeking a past life therapist.

Conventional therapies had not given Paula the answers she sought to her problems, and after spending many hours and a good deal of her resources with different therapists, she decided to try Past Life Therapy. Her primary concern was her aging mother, who was becoming increasingly dependent. Paula was highly attentive to her mother's health, making sure that she received appropriate medical care, but her anxieties about her mother's aging body had increased along with her fears of how she would cope with the loss when her mother died. These anxieties had become so severe that they had begun taking a toll on Paula's own health, through sleeplessness and other stress-related symptoms. Paula hoped that a successful past life regression would solidify her belief in the promise of an after- or next-life and that new-found faith would help her let her mother go when the time came, knowing that love might light the way for their souls to reunite in the future.

That was only a fraction of what Paula soon discovered. The remarkable story, which unfolded during her regression, gave Paula, *"So many answers to my difficult time with my mother and to all kinds of little questions about it."* Paula learned that she not only loved the soul of her present mother in a past lifetime, but also had actually caused her mother's past-life death! Once those unconscious memories were made conscious, Paula could finally understand and alter the powerful forces at play within the dynamics of their relationship.

The first images Paula saw of a past life in her regression were deceptively simple, until she looked below the surface. She was a sixty-year-old Chinese man working in a rice field, wearing sandals, pants and a loose shirt. Paula described his home and his life:

> There's a very small grass hut. It's a small room with a big door. The building is round. It's dark and cool inside, no artificial light. There's a grill outside made of metal and stone. Something is cooking, meat. It's good and hot. I'm very happy. I'm alone. I work for someone else, but I work for myself... I was sent there. I did something wrong when I was younger. I was sent away."

With that revelation, it became clear that this old Chinese man once led a different life before becoming a rice worker. Paula was instructed to go back to the time before he was sent away:

> I was young and rich. I wore a beautiful robe that was rich and heavy. I was in a court. I was arrogant. There's a pain in my chest. I like the wealth. I'm talking to people, bowing, but I don't care. I have a lot of rings. I'm dismissing people, waving them away.
>
> I'm bored, looking into another room at a woman. She's beautiful, a courtesan. I killed her out of anger. She wouldn't do what I wanted her to do. I strangled her and then I was very sad about it. I'm crying out of sorrow...
>
> People are taking me away. I wanted her only for myself. She couldn't because she was a royal courtesan for any royalty. She was rightful. My father was very angry. My choice was to become a peasant or stay and lose power. It was a great humiliation. I was disinherited...
>
> I chose to go out into the field. It was a good choice, more honorable. It was a happier choice. I found myself with the people in the fields. At the end, people would take care of each other.

The contrast between this man's youth and his later years was dramatic. Paula had no trouble seeing the purpose of that lifetime and how it related to her present life. She also received reassuring guidance about the separation she had so feared:

> To learn humility and that one doesn't have one's own way by taking someone else's life. It doesn't give you what you want. In youth, I was haughty, rude and self-indulgent. I had to learn that solitude is good. The woman I killed was my present mother. I had to keep on living

without her then, and now I do my best to keep her well and living in the best possible way. It's not going to be as bad as I thought. I killed her in the past because I wanted her for myself. My punishment then was to live with the pain of separation. Now I take care of other people, being the hand that someone else can hold.

From a wealthy, jealous lover to a repentant peasant and now a devoted daughter and nurse, Paula had journeyed far. Soon after her session, Paula sent an eloquent note of thanks:

Dear Amy, I can't tell you adequately what the reading meant to me. I spent time this morning meditating on it and the richness increased. I now have so many answers to my difficult time with my mother and to all kinds of little questions about it. After hours and hours with therapists and myself, there it was last night - so clear, so available. Thank you and your gift for helping me get closer to mine. I feel freer, more loved and more loving than I have for long time. And that's quite a lot to have gained. Thank you again. Peace, Paula.

The dual-gender nature of this regression revealed that in her life as a man, Paula went from being *"haughty, rude and self-indulgent"* to being a humiliated outcast who eventually found happiness in a solitary life among peasants, where people took care of each other.

Seeing the transformation that was possible within her, as a man, Paula was better able to view men as being capable of change. By softening her judgments of men, she was then able to share a softer, more attractive side of herself with them, and express the same qualities she had found attractive in the courtesan in her prior life.

Paula's unconscious remorse from the past had caused her to suffer enough and she no longer needed to deny herself the love she needed. She once again felt worthy of finding love and that liberating feeling would help her to release her mother in grace, thereby doing what she/he had failed to do in the past and close the circle in love. The calm solitude that brought peace to this Chinese man was now Paula's to reclaim whenever anxiety might appear. And, as she wrote, that's quite a lot to have gained.

Still Suffering from Old Taboos

If you have ever been socially ostracized for something you did, you know how hard it is to rise above the shame of tribal rejection and carry on with your life. Now imagine that you were experiencing that paralyzing sense of shame and remorse, except that you had done nothing socially inappropriate to make you feel that way. That was Hazel's dilemma.

After fourteen years of marriage. Hazel was struggling to decide whether or not to have a baby and didn't understand why she was so hesitant. Her marriage was fairly happy, except that she felt something was missing and wondered if it was children. She couldn't shake her fears of parenting and hoped seeing a past life would help her resolve her fears. She regressed to 1838 in a western town, and saw herself as a black man, age 38, in full clown garb, wearing clown shoes and red and white pants.

> No one's around. I live in a little shack with a window, a bed and a little table. It's messy in there. I have a small calico cat named George. He has a bell on. Not much electrical, everything's simple. I made a living as a clown, making people laugh with funny dances...

> I see a child, a nine-year-old girl in a hood. She has a white face. She's my daughter. Her mother and I are distant from each other.

Hazel went back farther in time in that life to see why he became a clown, and how he and his wife eventually met:

As a kid, I was beaten. I wasn't going to be beaten up anymore and I knew I was going to be independent...

I met my wife at a dance with a wooden floor. I thought she was pretty. Her name was Betty. We had a brief courtship, then I got her pregnant. I didn't know my daughter very well. She didn't know I was her father. It was such a lonely life. I died at 89.

It appeared that an inter-racial affair had taken place, which resulted in a daughter that Hazel was not allowed to know. When reviewing the purpose of that lifetime and its relationship to her present lifetime, Hazel saw a number of connections:

I know that I could survive. I was lonely then but I'm not so lonely now, but I'm still making people laugh. Then, my father made people laugh, but he was mean. He didn't really know me either. My daughter then was really sweet, but she didn't know me. That was really sad.

Due to the social taboos and circumstances of that former life, Hazel had carried his shame and remorse into this lifetime as an unconscious barrier through fourteen years of her present marriage. In perspective, Hazel saw that her loneliness in her former male life was a result of being denied the privilege of knowing her child; her present loneliness resulted from denying herself the pleasure of becoming a parent, because of her feeling of unworthiness.

Toward the end of her session, Hazel felt the psychic presence of an infant soul whom she sensed was her future child. Reaching out to it psychically, Hazel told the soul that this time she would be there, unlike before. Finally, Hazel felt she could allow herself to become pregnant, knowing she would love and cherish the child. Now she could experience not only parenting, but as a woman, she would also know the joys and pains of pregnancy and labor. Realizing this new soul was more frightened of being born than she was of becoming a parent made Hazel realize that her love for this soul would carry them beyond both of their fears.

CHAPTER FIVE: THE NEED FOR LOVE

The need for human love is universal. But too often we are the ones who keep ourselves from experiencing the love we crave because we have stopped feeling worthy of it. When deprived of love, we fail to thrive and it may take lifetimes for us to understand and honor that simple truth. The dual-gender stories that follow all have this common thread.

Guilt Drives Fear

What if the things we fear will happen to us, already did happen to us in a previous lifetime, but we don't consciously remember? We may remain haunted by unresolved issues these events represent, in search of soul forgiveness or healing from pains we may have once caused or suffered. This was true for Carol, an attractive and intelligent woman who at the time of her session was suffering from two irrational fears. One was that her husband, whom she loved and knew loved her, would *"turn away from me and leave me."* The other irrational fear was of *"not living out an entire life."*

Her first apparently groundless fear had become so acute recently that Carol suspected something in her deeply unconscious mind was causing it to persist. She knew that this anxiety if not quelled could self-fulfill as her husband grew tired of her paranoia, which was leading to a predictable disaffection.

Carol briefly reviewed three fairly uneventful lifetimes during her session, one of which was as a woman. The other two, described below, were male lives wherein family and love were absent. Both men died young. In her first male life, she described being barefoot on a dirt ground, wearing a heavy metal top that covered his whole body except for his calves and part of his arms. His name was Raphael and he was thirty years old, living around 1800:

There's nobody around. There are spurts of vegetation, it's out west. I'm riding a white horse. I have no provisions.

By the description of Raphael, he might have been a warrior or knight on a mission. Asked about how Raphael felt about his situation, Carol said in flat voice:

I don't feel anything. I'm in a small town. There are a lot of people around, doing their business. Nobody notices me. I unsaddle and hook up my horse and look for a place to stay. I go up to a room, lie down and go to sleep.

So far, Carol had not described any interpersonal relations, and Raphael seemed indifferent about being so alone. I instructed Carol to move ahead to the next significant event. Instead of going forward some hours, weeks, or even years within that life, Carol advanced to another male lifetime, which she described in brief overview at an emotional distance:

I'm on a train, age 35, in a suit, headed to California to make money... I'm working.

Carol soon saw that the man died young, although she didn't see a specific cause. Looking back from outside the body, Carol reflected:

I didn't find what I was looking for. I'm sad about it, about not finding love or inner peace, and realizing that money doesn't get you anywhere. My inner soul always lacked love, so I was glad to die.

This message about love was a powerful one, that we find our way to love or peace only by realizing that love and peace are the way. When asked the purpose of that lifetime, Carol saw that both male lives were devoid of intimacy in relations:

To learn, love is important. If you don't have it, you grow old and die.

Without love, we do indeed *grow old and die* even at a young age. As always, it is vital that a person understands how the incarnation just reviewed relates to the present. When asked about the ties, Carol's guidance was:

I must not waste life on making money and striving for material goals or take things for granted. If I don't love myself, then there's no love possible with others.

This basic message for Carol was one that clients often receive during this portion of regression sessions. When the soul reflects on missed opportunities that were allowed to slip away, it was her choice as to whether or not she has loving relationships and a full life. By seeing that she died young in the past, having left family ties behind prematurely, Carol understood that she had been carrying an unconscious guilt from the past, which she had been projecting onto her husband. This guilt dictated that her husband would want to abandon her.

By uprooting the source of her fears, Carol could release them knowing that her husband did not need to recycle her own past behavior, when she was a 'he'. Carol now also understands that the length of her life matters less than the peace and love with which she fills it.

Family Ties

Life changes may come easily for people who thrive on periodic upheaval and uncertainty. Others find the prospects of radical change more threatening than appealing. This was Emily's situation, until she realized through past life therapy that the change that beckoned her was really a familiar one.

Emily was an attractive divorcee with a young son and daughter. At the time of her session she was struggling with a romantic conflict. A new man in her life was very different from her husband and was urging her to radically change her lifestyle by selling her house and moving with him to a less populated and more natural setting. Emily worried that such a fresh start might not be the right decision, knowing that it would uproot her children. She hoped a past life regression would put these swirling changes into a more spiritual perspective. She regressed to see herself as a little boy named Thomas, who at age six, was already quite mature and, sadly, near the end of his life:

> I live on a farm someplace in the middle of the country. There are farms all around. I'm happy. I have a grandfather who I really love. My father was real big and tall and blonde. My mother was small with brown hair pulled back in a bun, like my grandmother. There are lots of animals around and a little baby girl. I love to be on the farm, doing the work, fishing and exploring. I love being in the woods and I could be happy either way, with the family or alone in the woods. I have no worries or fears or concerns...

> When my grandmother died, I was really sad. Then, I used to go away and not work as much and really be by myself. One day, coming home for dinner, some truck hit me and I die. I'm seven years old. My last thoughts and feelings were 'now I can be with my grandmother'.

The purpose of this young life was strongly connected to Emily's present life relationships:

> To learn about family. My mother then is my current daughter. It was hard for her, because I loved my grandmother so much more. She's returned because she loves me. My father from that life is my current

boyfriend. If I listen to him, he'll teach me about family. In this life, I am supposed to learn love, patience, humility and family.

Emily gave herself permission and courage to make a radical change. By seeing how much she as a young boy loved the excitement of the wilderness and farm life, she could embrace such a move as giving her current son the same opportunities for adventure. Emily cried during the session upon realizing that the soul of her current daughter was her former mother, returned to give Emily the love she was unable to give in the past. This was cathartic for Emily, who said that in many respects she felt that her daughter mothered her more than the reverse. Emily's Spirit confirmed that her lessons now are love, patience and devotion to family, as she felt in her heart.

Seeing her current boyfriend as her former father gave Emily trust and confidence to *listen to him* to learn about family. After this session, Emily put her house on the market and it sold quickly. She married her boyfriend and made a fulfilling family life on a New England farm.

The Long Lost Key to Commitment

In the natural order of things, most of us expect to find romance in our young adult lives, which should eventually lead to a serious, if not lifelong, commitment. If that presumed natural progression is out of order, it can be deeply disturbing to ourselves as well as to the people in our lives who love us and wish for our happiness.

That was what motivated Kelly to investigate reincarnation. Kelly, a beautiful and intelligent young woman by any standard, had achieved a fair degree of career success, working in a multi-media atmosphere that included radio, television and journalism. But she had not found happiness with a relationship, and wondered if unresolved issues from a previous lifetime were hindering her ability to make a commitment.

Making matters worse, her parents were pressuring her about her personal life. Kelly resented this meddling and had begun to avoid relationships just to defy her parents' wishes, a self-defeating spiral she wanted to break. Anger toward her parents was keeping Kelly from being happy with men who might actually become good marriage partners. She regressed to a very recent past life. She saw herself in the body of a ten-year-old boy named Tom, wearing sneakers, shorts and a shirt:

> I'm alone, looking around. It's swampy. I'm feeling bored as there aren't a lot of children around. I see an old white house and the front stairs are kind of broken and dusty. I live with an older couple, my grandparents. My parents took off when I was young — about five years old.

Kelly was instructed to go back in time, to see what led up to Tom's parents taking off and leaving him with his grandparents:

> They were too young to have a child. They didn't want the responsibility of a child, so their parents became my parents. I didn't like it. I'm very sad.

The rest of Tom's childhood seemed to provide him with a chance to make friends with nature:

> Over time, life improved. There had been neglect. I see animals. It was a kind of a farm. There were goats and chickens, cats and dogs. I cleaned out the barn, sweeping. I like all of the goats.

The next significant event came when Tom was an adult, at age forty. Kelly reviewed that event and the rest of the life:

> My grandparents just died. I had friends, but I never got married. There were opportunities to socialize, but I never wanted to make a commitment. I cared about them, but I

was used to feeling alone. Now that my grandparents have died, I feel empty. I fill the emptiness by socializing with friends. I keep busy, work and go to dances, and there is some romance. I didn't want to get married. I became more content with this decision... At the end, I see a small gravestone. I died of old age, of a heart attack.

Assessing the purpose of that lifetime, and its relationship to her present, Kelly saw some important links:

To learn self-worth. I was very strong and talented, but I doubted it. My parents in that lifetime took off. In this life, they stayed but had such a big family that I didn't get the attention I wanted. My parents abandoned me psychologically this time.   My father was always preoccupied with whatever he was doing.

Realizing her parents' problems were due to their own immaturity helped Kelly accept and forgive them. To avoid making their mistakes, it was important to her to achieve professional success and strengthen her self-worth before she could feel ready to commit to a relationship. In forgiving the past, Kelly also needed to acknowledge and forgive her own judgmental attitude toward her parents, who did their best.

Male or female, making and keeping a commitment requires the kind of maturity that Tom's grandparents had displayed, for which Kelly/Tom had been grateful. In addition to resenting her parents for neglecting her in this lifetime and the past, Kelly had unconsciously judged her parents to be unworthy of becoming grandparents, too. And, since she also judged them as having failed to be good parental role models for her, it was no wonder she was ambivalent about settling down to raising a family!

The dual-gender factor here was also playing tricks on Kelly's love life. Her unconscious memory of being a man who was romantic but not interested in marriage made her assume every man she met would feel the same way. Considering her past as a man who eschewed commitment, Kelly had a deep, unconscious sense of being unworthy of finding a man who was willing to commit. Bringing all this to the surface gave Kelly a unique and helpful perspective.

Since this session, Kelly has enjoyed continued growth in her career, as well as growth as a loving daughter toward her parents, who stopped applying any pressure on her. They trusted Kelly to be mature enough to know her own heart and mind, and to make whatever decisions are best for her. When Kelly was last heard from, she announced with delight that in the near future, she hoped to receive a marriage proposal from a wonderful man she was seeing, and that he had been worth the wait.

CHAPTER SIX: PAYING KARMIC DEBTS

Guiding a client in a past life regression is often like watching a soap opera play out, each lifetime a continuing episode of a karmic drama which might be called *"As the Wheel Turns."* The dual-gender cases in this chapter demonstrate the force of our karmic wheels and the greater force of grace, which enables us to stop the ride.

Opposite Pasts: An Executioner and Herbalist

The next time you are tempted to compare yourself to another and think, *"I'd never stoop to behaving like that!"* remember this story. As Diane learned through her regression, she was not as bad as her husband is now in one of her past lives, she was actually much worse! What Diane probably thought unconsciously all along in her marriage was *"I vow never to be that bad again!"*

At the time of her session, Diane was studying alternative medicine and planning to devote her life to healing, but knew she first needed to heal herself. She had been struggling with an unhappy and childless marriage of many years, wherein she endured frequent verbal and occasional physical abuse from an alcoholic husband. She hoped to learn through past life therapy why she felt so helpless to change her situation.

Diane reviewed two former male lives, which gave her a whole new outlook on herself, her husband and her situation. These males were extreme opposites: one a cold Executioner, the other a peaceful herbalist. She reviewed the herbalist lifetime first, although it came chronologically later than the executioner incarnation. They are described here in Diane's words.

The Herbalist

I'm in a field, like an Indian, picking flowers. I'm a little boy. I'm picking flowers to use for medicines and collecting them in my basket. I feel really good. I love the woods, the moss and the stream. I'm very happy.

There is an old lady in a big teepee. She will show me how to make herbal concoctions into medicines. She is a really nice old lady. I can talk to the animals. I love them and the earth. I feel so fulfilled, balanced and at home. I play and I'm learning to be at one. I'm full of love...

I die at age 73, as an old man. I know I'm going to die. It's not scary. I want to reassure those that love me that my spirit will be with them.

This gentle, male lifetime was like a soothing balm to Diane's soul. She said of her purpose in that lifetime and its relationship to her present:

The purpose of that life was to find beauty and to experience the joy of love and being balanced. The lady who taught me is someone I knew in my present life, when I was younger; she inspired me to love nature this time, too. This time, I am interested in herbs too, even though the mainstream culture doesn't understand them. That's part of what I'm doing now; helping to re-establish the wise use of herbal medicine.

Reviewing a male life so in harmony with nature reinforced for Diane the idea that all men are not necessarily as mean, selfish and abusive as her current husband. She had been using that stereotypical generalization to justify and overlook his abusive behavior toward her. The truth, she now realized, was that her husband was simply who he was, and not typical of all men. This helped Diane begin correcting her former mental tapes, which said she might as well stay married to him, since she couldn't expect to find another man who would be less cruel to her anyway.

As pleasant as that life had been, it offered little insight into why Diane's soul chose to suffer within the confines of her current relationship with an abusive husband. It was suggested that Diane remain open to her Spirit guiding her to review anything else which was relevant to her current situation. She then regressed prior to the herbalist to a very unpleasant male lifetime, where the seeds of her present marital karma were sown. It presented a stark contrast to the first soul:

The Executioner

I'm an executioner. I'm chopping people's heads off. I'm getting joy out of heads flopping in a basket... I've got a lot of power, but I'm afraid of death, afraid of the vengeance of all the souls I decapitated. I need to absolve myself. I go into a lake with clear water to clean my soul; I baptize myself, to rid myself of anger and vengeance... At the end, I'm being stabbed.

Diane lived and died by a blade in that life. Its lesson and how it related to her present lifetime was clear to her:

To know how power can be misused; I have to learn to be humble about power. My current husband was one of the men I executed. No wonder he never feels guilty for all the abuse he gives me! It's no wonder I keep feeling I should take it!

The enormous violence of her life as an executioner was shocking to Diane's rational mind, as she prided herself on being a pacifist and a humanist. To see herself having been an even viler male than her current husband helped her be less judgmental of him now.

She also realized that, just as the executioner chose finally to leave behind a violent life, so could she now. She understood that it was not up to her to reform her husband. He had to want to change. Seeing that in her present marriage, she was paying off a karmic obligation to a former victim, Diane could see that her marriage was not based on love but on his unconscious desire for retribution and her unconscious desire for redemption. Once Diane understood these dynamics, she was better able to understand her husband's abusiveness and adjust her expectations of him. Furthermore, having suffered enough, Diane could now feel more worthy of a loving relationship. Ultimately, Diane initiated their divorce, eventually finding a mutually loving relationship with a man who had no unconscious axe to grind with her! Another link between Diane's past and present is her career motivation and dedication to alternative medicine, stemming from her desire to minimize the need for surgery. The thing she most reviles today is the very thing she abused in the past. Having sliced off so many heads in the past, Diane now staunchly advocates avoiding *the knife* and trauma of surgery whenever possible.

From Brothers to Lovers

It is easy to judge a relationship from an outsider's view, using personal standards of what makes a good relationship work. However, not everyone enters a relationship with the same goals in mind, and in cases of couples that have been together in other lifetimes, their relationship goals may not only baffle the casual observer, but be completely unconscious to the two people themselves!

Kathy's relationship was a good example of this. Everyone told Kathy her relationship with Roger was too one-way, his. It was obvious to Kathy's friends that Roger did not deserve her devotion. As a result of her unselfish efforts, Roger's career as an artist was enhanced, yet little was received in return. Kathy never complained and was obsessed with a need to keep giving to Roger, who was perfectly content to use Kathy to his fullest advantage. Naturally, Kathy was confused, admitting that

Roger was too self-absorbed to attend to her needs. She wondered if this situation had past life roots.

The answer came as Kathy regressed to a life in France, during the time of Napoleon, where she and Roger were brothers. Because she immediately recognized Roger's soul as her brother then, Kathy continued to refer to him as *"Roger"* through the regression, although that was surely not his past-life name:

> Everybody's got powdered hair, wigs, fancy clothes. He's very famous as a court painter. I'm his little brother. We get along fine. He takes care of me. I'm a lot younger than he is by sixteen or seventeen years. He's sending me to school. He makes lots of money. Our parents are dead. They had money too. We have nice clothes and live in a nice house. It's very beautiful...

> I graduate from the university and I am traveling and going to other countries to act as an interpreter. We keep in touch. It's hard, because you have to write letters and it takes so long for the letters to get there and he travels too, so you don't know where to send the letters.

> I marry a girl from Italy. He's happy for me. He isn't married. He might be gay. We stay in France for a while, and Napoleon gets defeated and goes out of power, then everything is crazy. My brother can't find work. No one will pay a painter because he worked for Napoleon. He dies in England. I never saw him again. He dies in a street fight -- a hoodlum — someone tried to hold him up to steal his nice jewelry. They killed him.

> Then my wife and I go to Germany. I work as an interpreter, but she doesn't like it there. She gets homesick and wants to go back to Italy. We return to Italy, but don't stay long. We die in a fire at her father's house. The whole family dies; I can see the flames. We

had no children; we couldn't have children. We kept trying.

The purpose of that lifetime and its relationship to her present life was immediately obvious to Kathy:

> To become fluent in many languages -- seven languages. I've been told in this life that I speak French with an authentic French accent. My wife in that life is the same soul as a man I know now, who introduced Roger to me in this life. As my former wife, she took me away from Roger; now as a man, he reunited us. In that life, Roger had been devoted to me. When he needed me, I wasn't there for him.

Kathy saw that while her relationship seemed unbalanced to others, her soul needed to give Roger the same loving support she received from him as a past brother. Her feelings of kinship and obligation made her devoted to him regardless of how unworthy he seemed to others. Kathy linked Roger to prestigious institutions and contacts with people in positions to further his career. The satisfaction she received from these gestures, she now realizes, was tied to her unconscious need to compensate Roger for having abandoned him in those post-Napoleon years.

From brothers to lovers, Kathy completed her karma with Roger by giving to him, and in giving she received. While Kathy had previously assumed their relationship was destined to burn as a flame of eternal love, she now accepted that perhaps she might find more personal fulfillment with another man who was, after all, less self-absorbed. With her karma balanced, Kathy could finally let go of needing-to-be-needed by Roger.

Therapist, Heal Thyself

There are many ways of being ill and many paths to healing. When your body is ill, you consult a physician. If your soul is ill you may consult a psychotherapist or, like Ruth, a past life therapist.

Ruth was at a crossroads in career and relationships and was feeling disoriented. As a psychotherapist, specializing in helping women to heal the psychological scars of unhealthy relationships with men, Ruth had a big problem. She was involved in an affair with a married man. Worse yet, while she knew they had no future together, he was not her first entanglement with a married man.

Part of Ruth's attraction to married men was that they did not demand too much of her time, so her career could come first. Yet, the price she paid for this convenience was a great deal of inner turmoil. The hypocrisy of it all gnawed on her conscience, and the emotional dissatisfaction of loving men who weren't really there for her had begun to make the price of this freedom too high. She thought perhaps she should leave behind her career completely and make a fresh start working at something involving less emotional pain.

Ruth hoped delving more deeply into her unconscious mind through past life regression would clarify what direction would best meet her present needs. She reviewed a lifetime as a wealthy, forty-three-year-old Dutch man living in Spain, in 1492, wearing black shoes with buckles, stockings, a fancy lace-sleeved shirt and a black coat:

> I'm on a cobblestone street in a town. People are doing their daily things. I'm rich and very well thought of, dressed like a dandy with a pointed chin beard. People respond to me. They say good morning, like I've arrived. It's a nice day...

> I'm going to the office. I'm a doctor. It's a family practice, like a GP. The tables are wooden. I'll see about ten patients each day. I'm very happy. I love the children, the old women. I don't see any instruments. I talk to them, prescribe herbs, the right foods. I learned through my

father and at school, at Vandercook, Holland. I have no family life. I was an only child. My life seems to be my work...

I live to be 87 years old. I'm skinny at the end with a white beard. I'm comfortable; some children care for me.

While the details of that lifetime were fairly simple, it gave Ruth a good deal of insight to see that life's purpose and its relationship to her present lifetime:

To heal. To share and give of myself. As a doctor, I was free. I was like a flirt. I stayed unattainable for long-term relationships so that I could remain free. Now I always look for the unattainable - like married men - that's what I'm attracted to. I choose these men because they're unavailable, and that makes them more exciting. I don't even see the ones who are available.

Ruth's attraction to unavailable men was a carry-over from her past male life where she was unavailable to women. As a woman now, she can well appreciate the pain she/he had caused women in the past. By reaching this balance of understanding in her consciousness, Ruth was ready to break that pattern, to seek a healthier balance between career and relationships. She was ready to trust that she could commit to a relationship without sacrificing her career goals. Ruth's idea of freedom evolved beyond that of remaining free from commitment to being free to explore the dimensions of a mutually committed relationship.

The other connection between her past and present lifetime is Ruth's dedication to healing; then as a male physician and now as a female psychotherapist for women. Ruth fully appreciated the irony of the fact that, as a man who had been dedicated to physically healing people, he caused a great deal of emotional pain to women. These insights made Ruth recommit to her work, which she had considered giving up due to the conflicting feelings she now understood.

An added bonus Ruth received from past life therapy was a deeper appreciation for the roots of people's problems. Having healed her own psyche through past life therapy, Ruth had been introduced to a therapeutic tool she could now apply in her own work with women, thereby expanding her services to them even further than before.

Promiscuity; Mirror to Her Soul

"It hurts to be in love" begins a popular song that echoes a reality most of us face at one time or another when our love for someone is not reciprocated and the fall-out of love is harder than the fall into it. It is even harder to move on after a series of hurts and if we mirror each other's souls on the path of life, then what we find objectionable in others may be the exact same quality we once displayed by our own past behavior. Marie discovered that for herself through a past life regression. Marie was a sensitive woman who was a 'flower child' growing up and now wanted to be a productive part of society. Having come through the Sexual Revolution and the communal lifestyle of a large spiritual ashram, she was in a time of major transition. After college, Marie taught autistic children in public school but recalled being *"manipulated by the children."* She next apprenticed with a practicing masseuse, attended a massage institute and then went into private practice. She fell into a strange relationship with an unbalanced, manipulative *"psychic channel"* who so drained and confused her that she subsequently spent *"ten months vegetating in Santa Fe."*

Marie developed a dependency pattern where person after person took care of her until two consecutive houses in which she was living burned down, leaving her destitute. Abandoning her healing work, Marie started to waitress, and then joined the Rajneesh puram in Oregon for four years until it disbanded.

She met her current lover there with whom she was living within a communal house with friends at the time of her regression. Their relationship was unsatisfying and the household was breaking up. Marie had run the gamut between sexual extremes, from abstinence to promiscuity, yielding little satisfaction.

Marie wanted to dissolve the pattern of attracting men with whom she was incompatible and hoped past life therapy would help her understand why she had created this pattern of being attracted to men who were emotionally aloof yet who depended upon her for mothering. She hoped that if she could review a prior lifetime in which she knew true love, then she could hope to find her *"soul mate"* again in the present. Marie's regression demonstrated to her very clearly that irresponsible males who had hurt her in this life were a perfect reflection of her own past behavior as an irresponsible man in a former life.

Marie's review of a past life began as a sixteen-year-old male in Yugoslavia in 1842. Pausing at significant events to describe what happened, the picture she conveyed carried deep implications:

> I'm wandering around, avoiding going to school. I feel I already know far more than I could ever be taught. I live with my mother and several sisters, but I make very little contribution to them. Once, one of my sisters became ill, and that forced me to become emotionally involved at home. That was a brief but welcome change...

> In my mid-twenties, I got a woman pregnant and simply sent her off to my mother's. She left after five months, and I never saw her or the baby again.

> I finally had to work. I apprenticed with a cobbler. When I had to leave, I became a kind of roving cobbler, never settling down to establish a shop. In mid-life, I formed

one liaison with a woman whose children were already grown.

I died at the age of 78 with a small group of amiable companions around me.

Marie summarized her insights after reviewing the purpose of that life and its relationship to her present in terms of her soul's evolution:

> To learn that you get back what you put out. During most of that entire life, I never sought any responsibility. Only when circumstances forced me, did I get really involved in life. This time, I have to create something with my life... No wonder the man I am so attached to now is superficially affectionate but deeply cool and unresponsive: in this life, he is an exact mirror of the way I lived for an entire lifetime!

> Although I have a gift for intuitive healing, I have never become responsible for developing and sharing it. The only viable step for me now is consciously seeking out more responsibility, in work and in relationships. My soul is longing for intimacy, commitment and involvement. The question of parenthood, something I sidestepped in that life, is another possibility. In order to continue to grow and evolve, I must now move on from being a drifter. I must become deeply responsible for myself and for my life.

By seeing how unfulfilling her past life was as a male drifter, Marie knew she wanted to break that pattern. Her disappointments by similar men in the present brought her karma full circle, as she now understood the kind of pain she - as a man - had caused women in the past. Marie could now let go of the anger and bitterness she had felt toward this same type of man who mirrored to her how she had once been.

Another karmic link between these lives is responsibility for children. As a man, Marie had abandoned a child; in this life, Marie devoted her time and energy to working with needy children, although it proved a more difficult challenge than she expected. While it was not fulfilling work to her personally, it helped her balance a karmic debt that her soul had carried from the past. Marie soul's purpose in that life was a simple truth that transcends sexual identity: you get back what you put out. Though simple, its realization may take lifetimes to achieve.

> I see now that the man I have been so attracted to is superficially affectionate but deeply cool and unresponsive, an exact mirror of the way I lived for an entire lifetime! It's time for me to create something with my life. I have many gifts and talents to use. The next step is to seek out more responsibility in my work and relationships. My soul is longing for the experience of intimacy, commitment and involvement... also parenthood, which I sidestepped before; I'm open to it now.

Besides now understanding the pain she caused women in the past, Marie also saw that when women tolerate male irresponsible behavior, they contribute to and encourage that behavior, like an unconscious trap. From then on, as a woman, Marie would be more likely to recognize and reject unhealthy dependencies, knowing how they diminish our ability to grow, learn and evolve.

CHAPTER SEVEN: THE NEED FOR INNER PEACE

Inner peace may feel differently to different people, but we can all recognize when it eludes as we feel just plain *stuck* in our life struggles. This is one of the most common reasons people investigate past lives and as the following three dual-gender cases demonstrate, past life regression can be a powerful tool for helping individuals to recover the inner peace they needed.

Pride Gets In The Way

Sheri reported feeling just plain *"stuck"* with two problems at the time of her session: family communications, especially her negative relationship with her mother and how to improve her own coping mechanisms. She really wanted to make progress in these difficult areas, which made her feel incomplete and unhappy. She wondered if karma from a former lifetime was holding her back. Sheri discovered through her regression that these problems were related to each other and all within her power to effect. Sheri regressed to see a male lifetime in a desert area, more than a dozen centuries ago, in the year 500. S/he was a soldier in his mid-twenties, wearing sandals that laced around hairy legs and a kind of military skirt and breastplate. Sheri described his situation and the events that unfolded:

> I take orders from a fat, lazy-looking man. They are orders to create peace and enforce peace, but I use violence to enforce peace.

Asked about the root of the unrest that was preventing peace from existing and how he felt about his situation, Sheri said:

> The peasants violate the peace due to poverty and starvation. My thoughts are to be loyal to what I have to do, no matter what, even if I don't like it and what I see.

This seemed a lonely existence. When I asked Sheri about his family ties, the response was very cool:

> I have no family attachments. My family is far away. They're not bad off. I entered the military because that's what was laid out for me to do and be.

This mode of strict obedience to authorities would soon take its toll on this soldier. When Sheri was instructed to continue reviewing the lifetime and to pause when something significant took place, the next important experience was the following:

> I burst into a house with other soldiers and we killed a family. I felt horrible, but I did it anyway because I had to. I was alone that night. I wandered, and wanted to be alone.

> I didn't want to talk to anybody, so I could compose myself and come back. I was a good soldier, but I wasn't political enough to move up. I was dependable, did my job, and that was fine with me. That was the most horrible thing I did. I remember the look on the woman's face, the mother, when she was holding her child.

Not surprisingly, this soldier didn't survive into old age. When Sheri progressed to the end of the lifetime, the loneliness was again apparent:

> I was in my 40's. I died of a heart attack. Nobody was close to me.

Reviewing this lifetime encompassed by the light of Spirit, Sheri's newly won perspective was wonderful. She described clear links between the soldier she was then and her present life situation:

I was compassionate, but felt I had no control over what I had to do. I still think I don't have control over situations. The father, who I had to answer to then and hated, is my present mother. This time we have to resolve the power/control thing between us. We couldn't do it man to man, but maybe we can do it female to female. We're both egos filled with pride. Once that can be put down, the true balance can exist. We could let ourselves feel our love for each other if we can relate to each other honestly with no cover-up, shame or fear of consequences.

This session motivated Sheri to let down some defenses and begin communicating with her mother. She knew that as two women now it was more conceivable than when they were men. By overriding her pride and obeying her own heart, Sheri could dissolve the obstacle to her peace.

A Holy Man's Message

Amidst the constant bombardment of commercial messages we receive via print, radio, television, junk print and now even electronic mail, it is easy to lose sight of our values beyond material possessions. Patricia reclaimed a more simple set of values through her past life regression, by hearing a message that was strictly non-commercial.

Patricia was curious to know if some of her personality traits were based in past lives, including a fondness for spicy food and an attraction to bodies of water and languages. She also wanted to break a heavy cigarette smoking habit, but felt the stress in her marriage made it too difficult for her to give up the pleasure she derived from smoking.

Patricia reviewed a past lifetime as a twenty-nine-year-old man named Jarrod in about the year 929, in Palestine, wearing sandals on hairy legs, and a tunic:

I see sand and rocks. There are some crude wooden fences and a wooden bucket. The land is flat and rocky. There's not much life. My hand is on the fence, holding a piece of wood. Way over to the horizon, some green mossy grass is growing. I'm going to go there...

I have a big stick in my hand. I walk with it. I'm walking along this very narrow stream to get to the other side of the stream where the grass is, eastward. I'm walking faster.

I need to get someplace. I drink some water. It's cold. I'm dusty. There's a town or city, a big town. It's down the stream that goes over the hill, but it's not a waterfall. It goes into the earth, underground. This looks like Palestine. There are no trees. People are moving around here and there, not too many people. It looks baked. I'm going down the hill...

I'm in a passage between the buildings. They're crude, dusty and yellow. Someone is on the roof doing something. Birds are on the roof. They scamper away. There is a doorway, cool, dark, cavernous, with some tile around the edge of the floor, like a border. It's a temple. It's old. There is a shape. I can't see the shape. I'm looking for someone. It's a woman. She has a headdress on, a gold half-moon halo. It's a physical one, not glowing. She's got black hair and a long robe. She looks like she's from a bible movie. My stick's gone. She puts her hands on my shoulders. I'm much bigger than she is. I'm very muscular. I have a beard and curly hair. I've got so much hair, sandy color and green eyes. I'm rough and dusty and strong. I'm drawn to her.

She's married, but I would like to have her forever. She's playing with me. She doesn't feel the same way about me.

She desires me, but I don't have money. I can't have the woman because she's rich and dressed and perfumed. She's attracted to my ruggedness and my independence, but she wants more than that. She's very rich and won't leave her powerful husband. I'm not ashamed to be dusty in front of her. I still feel that I could have her...

People are suspicious of me. I'm a holy man, here to deliver a message. Children come up to me in an enclosed square. Mothers try to take them away. I smile at the children. The children come. The women peek. Men are under eaves in the shade around the square. There's a wheel that's going around to wind something or sharpen something. The men have these things on their heads, the white rags with the cords around them. I approach one man in the open air, under eaves. I'm asking what he's doing and why. He wants to know who I am. I tell him I've come with a message. He thinks I'm crazy but he wants to know. He's curious anyway.

The message is to get rid of things. The gold, they all want gold coins. The gold's power is its shine. But it's just like stones. I say to leave the gold. I don't want the gold. Gold is used temporarily. Stones are permanent. I tell them to stop what they're doing and listen to me. Gather your children and women. Gold is temporary. The stones are permanent...

They don't listen and the rich woman in the window is laughing at me. It doesn't hurt. I feel sorry for her. She's shallow. The people are under her power. I tell them to put down their wheel and leave their gold, and to drink from the water from the stream, the stream that doesn't reach the village...

I'm going back up and drinking from the stream. I've left them. I'm up high now. That big stone with the fence place is gone. I'm way up high. There's an ocean there. The stream is gone. I've left the body.

From her perspective outside of the body, Patricia could look over that lifetime and see its purpose and how it relates to her present:

To listen, to listen, to leave the gold. To transcend even the most beautiful things, like in my home, my Persian rugs. The spirit transcends. No one from then carried over in my present life. Few people are on the same wavelength with me. Like then, people don't listen.

Patricia satisfied her curiosity about a past-life cultural connection and was given a valuable message. The woman to whom Jarrod was attracted but who scorned his lack of material wealth was a mirror of Patricia at the time of this session, clinging to an unhappy marriage out of a desire for financial security. This was Patricia's situation, although because she was employed, she was not totally dependent upon her husband.

Jarrod's message to the Palestinians was just the advice Patricia needed. To follow Jarrod's advice and to trust that she would be all right if she dissolved her marriage was a test of her faith in powers beyond gold in the present.

While her marriage was not the primary focus of the session initially, it became so upon this review. Soon after that session, Patricia joined a smoking cessation support group where she found the help she needed to get control of that destructive habit. Once in control of that unhealthy aspect of her life, she gained confidence in her ability to be in control of other areas of her life. A separation and divorce followed not long after and her friends could only marvel at the tremendous change in Patricia that her new freedom seemed to create. Patricia, like Jarrod, was alone but whole and at peace within herself.

Life After Suicide

It is never easy to lose a loved one after spending years getting to know his or her special personality traits and habits and engaging in the wide range of give and take that make each relationship unique and memorable. Eventually the grief subsides as fond memories take the place of the presence of this person. Hard as this loss is, it pales when compared with the anguish a parent suffers when they lose a young infant or baby whose life held a world of promise and hope for the parent and whose death leaves a void that is extremely difficult to fill. That was Sharon's loss and still her primary sorrow after many years of grieving.

Sharon was a cheerful woman who loved life. She was happily married to her second husband and the mother of four healthy children who made her life very full. But she had known a devastating loss, the death of her firstborn child by her first marriage, years prior to this session. Although she had moved on, she still mourned that child and hoped the regression might bring greater understanding and peace about her destiny. She reviewed a lifetime as a native African male, which she described in excellent detail:

> I have bare feet. The lower part of my body is bare. I'm naked. I see lots of green trees and bushes. I have black skin. I'm standing in a funny pose. My left leg is down and my right leg is up. I'm doing a dance, holding feathers. I'm happy, joyful. I'm wearing a loincloth. No one else is here. I see huts made of straw, cone shaped. I have feathers in my head, bright colors. My left hand is holding a white feather and a rattle of some sort, a noisemaker. I don't have a spear. It's decorative. I'm celebrating something. A child is born. The mother and child are in the hut. It's my first child. It's a boy. It's just her and the baby in the hut. The village seems deserted. She moves around, touches the baby. She's very gentle.

Moving ahead in time, Sharon described how things began to unravel:

> Twenty years have passed, and I feel as if I'm being strangled. Someone is pushing be backwards. I'm decorated, with gold on my head. I'm falling backwards. My wife looks like a harlot. She's changed. My feelings toward her have changed. She seems hard and cold. The child didn't grow up. It died when it was little, in the cradle. The mother acts like she doesn't know it. She keeps bending over. She lost her mind. The village is split in half. No one is in those other huts.

For a better perspective on what occurred in the village, Sharon reviewed the childhood, including his bond with father, an important and powerful figure whose death was a major event. A woman named Camerra also played a critical role in his story:

> I'm 12 years old, with a bunch of boys on a river in a canoe, paddling. It's a team sport, a gang of us. I see a chief, an African with a big headdress, like a god. I'm not afraid of him. He's the boss. He seems kind, too. He's my father. He's bending over and patting me. He seems just to love me, with no expectations...

> Now he's turning white like a cloud, disappearing. I feel very sad. I'm very alone. I go wandering along, grieving. I'm picking berries off bushes. I'm dying in the grieving. I'm crawling along through the bushes. I keep winding around, almost like a snake...

> I stand up under a waterfall and start to feel alive again, part of nature, at one with the universe. The water washes everything horrible away. I feel strong, like part of the mountain...

I'm 19 or 20. I've grown powerful, like a leader. I have something to do. I have to go back. I'm taking my time going back. I'm not in any hurry. I have to think, to form a new concept of who I am. I have to think about what I have to do and how to go about it.

I see images of red. My tribe needs a sense of spiritual direction. My father was a spiritual leader. He glowed like he had the holy light on him. I carry that light. I can feel it; I have the glow on my head...

Back in the village, a lot of children are playing and swinging. No one seems to take much account of me. I enjoy watching the children. They seem so happy and free of worries. There's a big tree in front of me, a lollipop-shaped tree. I go to that tree. The tree is a sacred place. It holds some sacred meaning. It has a halo effect. I sit down. This girl comes over. Sometimes she seems like a squaw more than African. She looks at me. She's sitting down. When I look at her, sometimes she looks beautiful and sometimes she looks evil. Her face turns into a corpse-like look, with long black stringy hair. Her name is Camerra. When she looks away from me, she's like another form; she becomes transformed into something horrible. She wants to be friendly; she has desires on me...

I'm getting light again, from the bottom up. There's a huge celebration fire. We're all around it, dancing. There are about fifty people. We're holding hands, going in a circle. I'm married.

Everybody's small. Camerra goes off to the side. I'm with her. We're watching. She's like the devil coming to destroy me, but I don't know it. I'm led out into the bushes. I have an affair with her and she becomes pregnant. Evil is trying to consume me. It's so sad to come back with so much hope and be led away so quickly. Two things are going on, simultaneously. I have a wife and she's having our baby, and this other horrible woman is leading me away. I love my wife. I'm trying to kill myself; I feel like I'm trying to stab myself. I feel it in my heart, a pain in my heart. I feel like my life is of no value, wasted.

I'm ruined, totally lost. I stab myself. My wife drags me back to the hut. She cares for me. The baby is not born yet. My wife doesn't know that I've violated our marriage. She's not judging me...

There's a funny face there I can't place. It has long stringy hair. Somebody's head was left to rot, a dead face with hair on it -that woman. Her hair is the same. Her face is all rotted. I'm still lying in the bed, being nursed. This is happening at the same time. The light comes again. I want to keep that head to remind me of the dangers of evil.

The gift of Camerra's shrunken head seemed to evoke a sense of victory for him, although he did not see who was responsible for this gift. The assumption was that because he, metaphorically, lost his head over Camerra, she thus, literally, had to lose her head so that he could recover his. After that episode of Camerra's beheading and his suicide attempt, he calmed down considerably and turned toward higher pursuits:

My wife is older and wiser. We have to be together. We've had too many hardships. She was preoccupied with the baby. We're alone. I'm on a spiritual mission and she's with me. We're not going anywhere. We see light and power, sitting there in tune with something.

Unlike the first suicide attempt, which was clouded by shame and remorse, his next suicidal effort was an enlightened event under different circumstances. It was successful:

> I'm pretty old. My hair is grey. I'm alone now. My wife died. My body was consumed by fire. It was self-inflicted. There was no fear or terror.

Sharon was able to assess how the purpose of that lifetime related to her present, going beyond seeing evil as embodied by a temptress, to understanding how the choice is always — and only — one's own to make:

> Purity, the highest form of purity; to seek the higher level like a bird. When I reach the spiritual, there is a tremendous flood of light trying to reach up, lighting everything. In the past, I didn't use my light to help others. I wandered as a hermit. The power under the waterfall was about leading and guiding. But I was led astray by that evil woman, and felt I had to continue alone since I was attracted to the evil. The only way I could keep the evil away was to be alone. In this life, I keep denying evil in people. I don't want to see evil in people. It's painful. I keep seeing that girl's face turn back and forth. I don't want to see people's evil side. I had the power and I felt the holiness. When I met her, I turned off the light and said, I'll be just a man. I didn't want to deal with the responsibilities of the light. I didn't let the light work for me. I didn't want to keep the light on. I turned off the light to pursue the lesser side; when I turned it off, I walked on the evil side and I relinquished something. It took a long time to get the light back. A lot of horrible things happened ...fifty years of living, isolating myself. I wanted the light back. It was living in hell, my punishment for doing something in my youth for power. In my old age, I sought oneness. I should have been a

leader as a youth to achieve unity and oneness with God. At the end, I didn't care about people. I didn't care about eating. I was shrunken and frail and starved myself to death. I didn't want to lose the light. I kept drinking but stopped eating. I still have a desire for the light.

Sharon then integrated with the light of her own Spirit and received the healing she needed regarding her deceased daughter, whose angelic Spirit spoke to her, bringing with it a tremendous sense of inner peace:

I see the Spirit of my daughter. She was a light given to me, to lead me to think of thoughts of God and to get my mind back up into the heavens. Through her death, I had to deal with so many issues again. She's saying, "It's okay, Mommy. I'll keep leading you." I keep seeing this light upwards; I have to keep reaching up. Before she died, I was always afraid of myself. I thought I was weird. I didn't trust myself inside. After her death, I had to learn to trust myself. I'm not as afraid now to walk into realms of uncertainty. I'm okay, I won't get lost in the unknown. There's always someone to lead me back to safe ground. I'm not alone.

Sharon found meaningful connections between her past life as a man whose only child died, and losing a child in her present life. This time Sharon did not give up but went on to bear and raise four more wonderful children. In a real sense, the loss of her first child gave Sharon a much greater appreciation for the health and individuality of each of her other children, whom she loves unconditionally and joyfully. Sharon's encounters with the contrast between the guiding light and tempting evil reinforced some of her present beliefs about her own personal quest for spirituality and the leadership responsibility that comes with that gift. The search for inner purity was an important theme for Sharon, carried over from that life, when s/he projected good and evil onto women. As a woman, Sharon knows that we each have these qualities within us, as complex human beings with a full range of emotions and aspirations.

CHAPTER EIGHT:
HEALING THE TRAUMA OF RAPE

Past Life Therapy work often involves locating the unconscious roots of clients' deeply ingrained problems, then introducing the necessary alchemical ingredient that will release them from their suffering, such as forgiveness. This dual-gender story is a good example of an individual for whom past life therapy was a vehicle for healing.

Rape. Few other words have the same power to evoke an emotional response of outrage accompanied by images of cruelty, inhumanity, injustice and disgrace. Yet, for those whose job is to provide emergency care to women who have been victims of rape and who are in a state of shock, it is vital to maintain a state of emotional calm. The emergency care physician must convey a degree of professional, clinical detachment in order to assist these women in getting the attention they need to cope with their losses and to move on with their lives.

Usually, that was not a problem for Dave, who was a competent physician in a hospital emergency ward, specializing in shock and trauma. But lately he had been finding it hard to separate his own feelings from those of his patients. Nothing in his medical school training had prepared him to feel so vulnerably empathetic, and he was afraid that his medical judgment might become impaired if he did not get these unwelcome emotions more under control.

Dave shared this difficulty with his hospital colleagues, hoping to find a base of professional support to help him understand what he was experiencing. But to his further confusion and aggravation, he met only unsympathetic and skeptical responses. This led him to wonder if his colleagues were too afraid to confess to having had similar feelings or if he was on the verge of a nervous breakdown due to the stresses of his job, as they implied by their judgmental attitudes. Dave hoped to find a better explanation through investigating reincarnation, and tracing the roots of his problem to something deeply unconscious within a past life experience. As with many clients who approach past life therapy, Dave had found other avenues of healing to be unsuccessful and figured he had nothing to lose. At the start of his session he indicated that, besides wanting to find a reason for these irrational emotional responses to his patients, he also wanted to understand what he called his *"karma in love."*

Dave learned in regression that he had experienced similar traumatic events in a previous life, which explained his stressful reactions to the women he was treating in the hospital emergency room. He regressed to a lifetime in France in the mid-1300s, where he was a young woman of 18 or 19 named Miriam. Dave saw that Miriam was wearing *"primitive shoes, sandals, a robe and no underwear."* The awareness of Miriam having no underwear on was foreboding of very bad news. Miriam's village was under attack by a group of missionaries:

> I was raped and tortured by a group of soldiers who also killed my whole family.

At the moment of recognition of what had happened to Miriam, Dave experienced the same sensation of traumatic shock that he had so often encountered in his hospital emergency room patients. Only this time, Dave wasn't just feeling for a victim; his feelings were those of a victim.

Words could not do justice to the intensity of Miriam's pain and suffering or to Dave's relief at uncovering the answer to his question. It was very emotionally satisfying for Dave to achieve a sense of vindication, that his recent hypersensitive responses to rape victims had good cause.

In cases where a client immediately regresses to a highly traumatic event, it is common to guide them to review earlier times in the life to see what preceded the event. Scanning Miriam's early years, Dave saw that her youth had been hard, coming from a large family where:

There was never enough to eat. There was social disruption, superstition and death from disease and war. Several of my brothers and sisters died young of common childhood diseases and only four survived into their teens. Our family is basically Catholic; we're pretty superstitious. My people are not very bright.

After bearing so many children and struggling to meet basic needs, it was no surprise that Miriam's mother's body gave out. After she died, Miriam's father was fortunate to remarry a woman who carried on with the necessary domestic activities. Miriam felt close to her brothers and sisters, and even recognized the soul of a then-brother as a being a present-life cousin with whom Dave was a very close playmate growing up. When asked what Miriam enjoyed, Dave saw:

Fields of flowers outside the village give me pleasure.

Before closing, Dave returned to the end of that life and beyond the death. As to the purpose of that life, Dave saw:

To experience mindless hate and pain, and to learn not to consume people as if they're inanimate objects. Everyone has memories, feelings and simple pleasures.

This was profoundly meaningful relative to his being a physician in an emergency ward for shock and trauma victims, where he must be conscious of how others feel and empathize with how he affects them both as a person and a doctor. Summarizing how this past lifetime relates to his present:

There are many kinds of rape. I've worked with many women who have been raped, and seeing myself as a woman gives me an understanding of women's feelings that has stayed with me as I work with women, an insight, and a little more balance. I see things differently than my fellow males.

Dave actually reviewed three lifetimes in the same session. In the others, he was a male doctor and priest with many more meaningful connections to his present life. Only in the female life, however, did s/he live in the shadows of others' needs and desires, and experience being a victim of violence. Dave's new understanding of his hyper-sensitivity at work gave him permission to grieve for the women he served who were victims of the same senseless violence he now realized he too had once known. Now as a man, Dave is dedicated to helping women heal the wounds of rape, providing the kind of service that was unavailable in the past, thus turning past a former helplessness into effective action now.

Dave realized his *karma in love* was to commit to sharing a loving relationship with a woman as his equal in his personal life. He understood better after his session why so many women didn't easily trust men to have and/or fulfill so noble an aspiration.

CHAPTER NINE:
FRIENDS, LOVERS AND BETRAYAL

To establish and sustain an intimate relationship takes at least two vital ingredients: good communication and trust built on a perception of mutual loyalty. Without these, the odds of achieving true intimacy are diminished.

Sometimes, we carry into present relationships unconscious memories of betrayal from former lifetimes. When this happens, remnants of unresolved anger often motivate us to behave in destructive ways that work against building harmonious relationships and instead create confusion and frustration for both partners.

Jane sensed there were hidden dynamics in her relationship with Ned and wanted to understand them. Lately, she found herself prone to exaggerated flare-ups of temper toward Ned which neither understood. Their bond was tremendously psychic; Jane could feel Ned's presence just by thinking of him and they sent and received psychic messages back and forth with little effort. Jane loved Ned but wished he would trust her to share more of his feelings. Jane was doing her best to share her feelings with David, but wasn't always sure he wanted to know about them. Jane often felt a need to test Ned's loyalty, although he always seemed to pass her tests. This made her wonder why she was suspicious in the first place. Worse, she realized that her suspiciousness was beginning to drive Ned away.

Due to his disastrous first marriage, Ned was afraid of commitment and often pushed Jane away just when she was sure he needed her the most. This was difficult for Jane, who wanted a full-time commitment and was completely clear about the intensity of her feelings for Ned.

Because Jane was so eager to know if the strains in their relationship had past life roots, she was a good candidate for regression. She found herself in the body of a hungry twenty-five-year-old Italian man named Salvatore, in 1637, wearing black shoes, pants and a shirt. He was in a noisy market place, looking for fruit among fruit-and-vegetable carts, chickens, meats and crowds of people when the story begins to unfold:

> There's a woman running after me and she catches up to me. She's angry with me because I left her back there and I didn't tell her where I was going.

Jane was instructed to go back in time, before he left this woman, and to describe what made him leave:

> I'm in a field and I'm working as a farmer. I'm working with grain in the field. Then, I'm coming back to the house and I'm coming in the house but she's not there, and it's dinnertime and I'm hungry. There's another man coming out of my bedroom, and she was there with him, and I'm hungry and there's no dinner.

When asked who the man was and how Salvatore felt:

> He's got the farm down the road, he lives down the road. When I leave, I go out to the field to a place under a tree and sleep under the tree, but not very much, because I'm angry. I don't know who to be angry at - her, him or myself. We'd been married about three years. We had no children. She cleans the house and cooks and tends to the chickens. There's not much passion.

To learn if their affections for each other had somehow changed over time, Jane was asked if they had been passionate during the earlier courting period:

> Not very much. It was an arranged marriage and she was very young and very pretty. We had some communication but men don't really discuss much with women.

Continuing to review that lifetime:

After that, we're still married. She's had a baby. I'm not sure if it is his or mine. She's not sure either, so it's upsetting. I'm expected to take care of them and provide, but I feel like I've been duped, taken advantage of; I'm not sure I ever trusted her, so that hasn't changed. I'm always worried that I'm going to find her with somebody else. All three children look like me. The relationship grows comfortable, like friends.

Salvatore died at age 42, which didn't seem young at the time. He and his wife were in a boat:

I drowned in a boating accident as we were going across the river. She died too. The children got out okay. They didn't die. Two were with us.

When asked the purpose, or soul lesson of that life, Jane's guidance was simple and practical, reflecting Salvatore's attitude:

You can't make things always the way you want them to be. You have to take them the way they are.

Jane now was clear about how that life related to her present relationship with Ned and the many dynamics that were hidden to her before:

Ned was the other man. He was my friend and neighbor. I kept quiet about it, but I always wondered after that. There was some anger. That may be the reason for some of the seemingly stupid things I've done in our relationship in this life, things I can't explain otherwise. He violated my space then. Ned thinks I always want things to be the way I want, but that's not so. I try to be what people expect, to fulfill their expectations of me.

Seeing that she and Ned were male friends in that life before the infidelity gave Jane a new perspective for Ned's present karma. Knowing how isolated both men became after that incident was in itself enough punishment for Jane. Also knowing that Ned already had suffered terribly by a first failed marriage made Jane want to forgive him for the past and, as she did, the anger that had been fueling her recent temper flare-ups suddenly disappeared. Jane asked her Spirit for guidance about Ned and heard these words:

> This time we came together to experience joy. I should do whatever I can to enhance joy, relax and not be afraid to say I love you.

As a man in the past, Jane/he could not express feelings verbally. Now as a woman, Jane communicates her feelings well and sees the importance of being responsible for communicating even if her partner does not respond the way she wants.

Seeing herself as a former man gave Jane more empathy for the difficulty men have acknowledging their feelings. It increased her patience with Ned, with whom, as female/male friends and lovers, she explored a level of intimacy not possible as same-sex friends.

Once these previously hidden dynamics were made conscious to Jane, many subtle emotional shifts began to occur within her, as she started to see her relationship with Ned in a new light. She no longer felt the need to test his loyalty toward her, and began to feel more comfortable about the friendship aspect of their relationship. Ultimately, Ned and Jane went separate ways, as he was still not ready for the kind of commitment Jane sought. Jane accepted the relationship, her soul understanding that *you can't make things always the way you want them to be; you have to take them the way they are.*

CHAPTER TEN:
PATRICIDE AND THE COST OF HATE

When groups of souls reincarnate together from lifetime to lifetime, they often shift roles with one another, much the way a good theater troupe stays together through many plays, changing characters in different productions. That, among other things, was what Beth discovered through her past life regression.

At the time of her session Beth had been through a difficult divorce and was now a single mother, raising her young son alone. She was confused by her feelings about men in general and toward Jim in particular and hoped that reviewing her soul records would shed light on the roots of her problem. Beth said she felt no sense of her own power and her lack of self-confidence was the source of much sadness to her. The connection between her feeling of powerlessness and of being sad became very evident in the circumstances of the past life Beth reviewed.

When a soul needs healing because of a past trauma, the individual may regress first to the highly charged event. Beth regressed to an especially critical past life moment as an educated Jewish man in his 30s. He was a fighter wearing gold sandals and leg armor with a maroon and gold chest cover:

> I'm standing on sand and holding a sword that has metal with a decorative hilt in my right hand. It's about one and half to two feet long. I have blood on my hand. There may be some camels near by. I see some thatched structures but I don't feel any people around me.

To place this violent episode into a comprehensible context, Beth was instructed to go back to an earlier time in that life and review the events that led up to it:

> I'm about 7 years old, in a village. I'm happy, playing and wearing a white tunic and I'm looking for my family. We

live in a house in a dirt courtyard in Jerusalem in Biblical times. I see a longhaired woman who's wearing a tunic. My father isn't around.

He went off into the desert, but mother is staying strong and confident. There is a male teacher sitting with us boys, teaching us out of a book of some kind. It instilled in me a desire to travel... I see a horse. I'm older now, 19 and I'm riding off with some other young men. Mother's sad that I am going. I feel her sadness. We're off on a fighting mission. Our people have been wronged. It is a religious defense. We're a small village of a belief and we're going off to stop the Romans from wiping out our people. I'm riding out of the village and off into the desert; the sand is mixed with dirt. There are six or seven of us...

I'm in another village now, with stucco buildings with two levels. It's Spanish or Moorish and feels like northern Africa. We're very out of place and there are antagonistic reactions to us. We're riding through the market area and people are suspicious. We're talking to a large sheik in a Moroccan, Turkish and Arabic setting. There are angry words. He's laughing at our insignificant threats. He allows us to leave. Then, we're meeting with people in that city who are against him, talking about how displeased and disgruntled they are with him. I'm a ringleader in this endeavor. At the conclusion of the struggle with people of power, neither side wins. The regime is still standing. We reached a truce. My village was not hurt...

I'm in the desert now, with a lot of people wearing different colored robes. I'm in the middle of the circle, fighting with one other person to resolve the controversy. My hand is bloody from a wound on my arm. This person is very large with a dark beard, dark turban and flowing robes. I see so much hate in him. He's a really hateful person. I don't want to kill him but I must to resolve the conflict. I'm much younger than he is. A lot of people are angry and yelling and throwing fists around. I see the same sandals and arm guards as at the beginning...

That awful person was my father. He had left the village to join these awful people. He had sold out. I see myself killing him now, right below his breastbone. He could have killed me if he'd wanted to. At the end, the hate in his eyes softens, from black coal to softer. He says my name at the end. I jam my sword down into the sand and walk away.

The crowd moves out of the way for me to walk through. My compatriots are happy... I go back to the village to my mother. She knew that's how it would happen. We're both crying and holding each other. But, there's a feeling of peace from the whole thing. We know everything will be all right now. I rode and rode and rode, and I'm screaming out from the pain and the hurt. He was a person I never really saw until I had to go fight him. I hated him for leaving.

Once Beth completed the story behind her first regression image, she was instructed to move forward in time to the end of that lifetime, to see what transpired since that violent episode:

I'm old. The village was saved. I have a daughter with me. My wife has died. I lost a son, but my daughter's with me as I'm dying. She has children and a husband. I'm important in the village, a patriarch. I'd gotten into some kind of a statesman position, but lived very simply in a hut like they all did.

Beth saw multiple purposes of that lifetime and asked for clarity about their meaning, so she could fully understand their relevance to her present:

> Cleansing... salvation... elimination... light as opposed to dark. It has to do with hatred from the loss. There was an incredible loss there, having to so terribly eliminate the cause of the loss. My father then is my mother now, the person from whom I feel such a lack and hate yet from time to time I want to bond with her.

> I had loved my wife very much. She was supportive and kind and loving, but I was always too busy... my wife then is Jim. I make myself really busy so I can't feel all the love he has for me. It was a Judaic village. My son now is the son I lost then to illness and grieved in that life. To be complete, I need to forgive and release, have more faith... faith to give me the grace to release and forgive and not hold onto the pain and hurt of abandonment.

Beth's male life was one of mixed messages. He was raised in a religion that values and preserves the family and community. Yet, his own father abandoned everything and even threatened the survival of the village and the religion. That situation forced a painful confrontation between the past and future, where the son's only choice was to kill the father who had become an enemy of his people. To make matters worse, Beth's own son of that life died, another painful loss within the Jewish faith, where the male lineage is so important to a father's peace of mind and sense of duty. Being male presumed an authority within the family unit, but the father's betrayal had turned the natural order of things upside down. Bern's soul had been powerless to change the situation, except by violating all that was sacred to Jewish religion, since the father was not worthy of being honored or obeyed.

Beth had made important progress toward understanding the complexities of her relationship with her present-mother/past-father. Seeing the bitter past bonds with this same soul, which ended in disaster, she was better able to accept their present, loveless relationship.

She was able to see that on a soul level, her mother was doing her best to make amends for having abandoned the past family, by coming into this life she as a woman and enduring the pain of childbirth and by undertaking duties of mothering. Beth could now see it as a noble attempt to compensate those who were abandoned in the past. It was easier now to forgive this now- woman/mother for not being talented at family relations and for not having a natural maternal instinct.

To learn that her present son is the same soul she lost as a son in the past was also an important revelation for Beth, and gave her a new perspective on her feelings about this son, whom she cherished above everything and everyone else. Unlike her own mother, Beth's feelings abounded with gratitude and love for her child and she now understood those differences on a deeper level. The insight Beth gained about her current relationship with Jim (past wife) created another bridge to a healthier, happier future. She had repeated an old pattern, of being too busy to allow his love in, but Beth wanted that to change. It was now clear that mutual love needs room to grow, which means taking time to show another you care by shifting priorities to be more inclusive of the other person.

Beth appreciated the ironic karmic balance she had achieved. In her past life, she was an absent father to a son, leaving the mother to raise the child, to pursue a fighter's mission. Beth is now a mother and primary parent, raising a son. As with the insight toward her present mother, Beth now can forgive her ex-husband and feel less victimized by her status as a single parent who was abandoned by a spouse.

CHAPTER ELEVEN:
TRUE BIBLICAL STORIES!

There is no book more widely read and discussed than the Bible. Bible stories offer us spiritual comfort, moral guidance and an appreciation for the hardships faced by our ancestors. For the three individuals whose dual-gender stories follow, the Bible now holds a more personal meaning, ever since each reviewed a past life during Biblical times.

A Spiritual Path

It is always fascinating to see how often our career choices reflect something connected to a past lifetime that we are drawn to repeat or fulfill in our present. In Jeanne's case, her work as a massage therapist for women turned out to have deep meaning on a soul level, as she discovered through her regression.

Jeanne said her primary interest in experiencing a past life regression was to further her spiritual understanding of herself and of life. She had no expectations, but was open to discovery. In this life, Jeanne has explored different lifestyles, including a conventional marriage and parenting, lesbian relationships and celibacy. She also wondered if she and her current female lover knew each other in a past life. She regressed to biblical times, to 3 BC when she was a seventeen-year-old male named Abe, wearing sandals and a cotton tunic with a rope around the waist:

> I live in the desert in a tent with holes on the outside. It's not big. There's a camel and other people around and I am a nomad. I don't eat much. There's a pot hanging over a tripod over a fire. In it is something that's cooked for a long time, meat and water soup.
>
> There's a bag on the camel. I don't do much. I don't have much ambition. Our family always lived here. My mother

is frail and drawn. My father is strong willed and keeps us here in this place. We don't know why, but we do. I have an older sister and a younger brother. As the older brother, I'm expected to do a lot. I have to do things my father ought to do. I think about not living there. When we meet other people, as we move from place to place, I want to live with other people...

At age 23, I'm married and my wife and I are in the city of Jerusalem with our two-year-old son, Jericho. My relationship with my wife is good. She's pregnant. I'm a carpenter and life is hard but we enjoy it.

As this regression took Jeanne back to biblical times, Abe was asked if he knew of Jesus. Jeanne said:

I was aware. I just know there is something greater that we can be and I try to be that. I look for the good in people. My heritage is Jewish.

Abe died before his wife after living what would have been considered a long life in those times. When Jeanne progressed to Abe's death, she saw that he was a man at peace:

I'm an old man. I had a grandson, but the child died in birth. It was hard on her body. I feel fulfilled. It was wise to come off the desert.

Looking back, after Abe's death, the purpose of that life and Jeanne's awareness of its relationship to the present was clear to her, especially regarding Abe's wife:

To improve the quality on earth, to lead a good and loving life, to add peace and harmony to the earth. There is sadness about leaving my wife. The spiritual aspects of that life and my present are similar in awareness; I'm continuing a path. My wife then is my current partner."

Jeanne's dual-gender experience of having lived as a man helped her further understand her present sexual identity and preference for women, especially for her current partner to whom she/Abe had been happily married and saddened to leave. Jeanne's present lifestyle reflected another significant tie; Abe's wish to leave the desert to go where he could have more contact with people. This struck Jeanne as ironic, because in her present life, she went to great lengths to live outside of the hectic bustle of the city, and is happiest in a rural setting. Jeanne lives in a similarly natural environment as Abe did, only this time she can walk for miles on sandy beaches by an ocean, instead of a sandy desert and enjoys more balanced contact with people.

Another thread connecting both lives was revealed to Jeanne at the end of the regression. When she saw Abe's grandson die in childbirth, she said 'it was hard on her body'. Abe had been helpless as a man to offer any intervention or support to ensure that his grandson's birth would be safe for him and the mother. This was a cause of great sorrow to Abe. Jeanne's current work as a massage therapist is primarily dedicated to providing women with the physical support they need to reduce stress and tension, making a great difference to women whose bodies need a loving, therapeutic touch. Jeanne knows she can give this supportive and healing touch, woman-to-woman, far more effectively than if she was a man.

On Noah's Ark

Who among us knows what lurks beneath the surface of each other's personalities? Sylvia learned some surprising things about what lurked far beneath her own surface, through a quite unusual regression whereby she also learned some remarkable things about her own psycho-sexual- spiritual nature. Before seeking out the services of a Past Life Therapist, Sylvia had spent years in therapy dealing with various issues and hoped now to find out if something from her past lives could contribute to the healing she still needed in the present. She also wondered if she knew her current husband and/or daughter in a former life.

Sylvia's past life review took her aboard Noah's Ark, a shocking story to spin the heads of theologians and historians alike. Sylvia's regression blended the themes of destruction, sex (or lack thereof) and the powerful force of nature. She landed on Noah's Ark, as one of Noah's sons. It was literally the original calm before the storm:

> The sun is out. It's time to leave. I feel good. Noah was a man of conviction and belief. He seems to know what it's all about, planning, organization and purpose. He's comfortable with what he's doing. He's a good father, easy to work for and be with. I'm feeding the animals grains. It's so nice and the sun is out and the air is good. Everybody is peaceful and content and so are the animals. We have everything, two by two. I'm going over the hill, exploring a new place.

Sylvia continued reviewing the voyage:

> The voyage was dark and dreary and wet. Noah kept the spirit together and courage high. There is a feeling of a higher purpose, even among the animals. We struggle, but it's not as difficult as one might have thought.

Given this rare opportunity to peer into the inner workings of an historic event, captured from the perspective of one soul's records, I asked what he felt for those who were left behind. Sylvia's response was very unemotional:

> It was the purpose, part of the plan. God loved them and it was fine. That was all that was important. Even then, I knew there would be more lifetimes. I was good and

content. Noah became old and died. He fulfilled his purpose. After he was gone, we lived separately. I only feel good. My wife died and I was left alone.

This was too neat and cozy for the kind of dramatic event one would imagine the story of Noah's Ark to be. What was the rest of the story? Returning to the voyage, Sylvia described how others aboard the Ark had managed the trip. Things there had indeed become rather messy and thereby more believably human:

> The wife of my brother didn't take the journey well. She wanted... she cared about me, but she was my brother's wife. It went unspoken. She was angry because of my conviction to follow the plan. My dedication to that, she called "single-blindedness". She drowned. She jumped over the side. That wasn't my fault. Nobody knew she was gone. I was so single-minded. I didn't understand and I couldn't divert my direction. It was wrong for me to become involved with her other than as her husband's brother. She had two children with my brother. I guess we helped raise them.

Noah's daughter-in-law being overwhelmed by it all and committing suicide overboard the Ark was a curious twist to the story. The details of what happened with her were sketchy but Sylvia seemed to suggest an unrequited love between them. Looking back, from the end of that life, Sylvia shared what she perceived its purpose to be and how it relates to her present:

> Fulfilling a commitment to Noah and above that, to God, to believe and listen to the message and follow it with strength and courage. He didn't look for an 'out' or wonder why, he just did it; to teach and share that conviction and knowledge; to be willing to share it without apprehension of what somebody might think or feel against or about me. It was part of the plan...

My present daughter was the wife of my brother. A girl I knew in high school was my wife then. In my head, I thought the life was very succinct and according to plan, but maybe it wasn't. Maybe I ignored those other things. Sexually, there wasn't much going on with me.

My drive to do what I thought was important took all my energy, drive and attention. As a consequence, certain aspects of my life were left undone. I'm doing the same thing now. I seem to let the purpose at hand crowd out my feelings; I take my pleasures from successive following through. I'm too busy. These efforts seem to replace or override any sexual needs. Fulfillment seems to come from the creative efforts, which replace sexual satisfaction with creative satisfaction. I don't want to stop that.

It was dawning on Sylvia that she didn't need anyone else's permission to find fulfillment through creative self-expression rather than through sexual relations. This was a good sign. When Sylvia asked for additional guidance from her Spirit about how to be at peace with her sexuality and her choices, she took a very wonderful, healing journey:

I see a cosmic sexuality, a brightness and a physical sensation. There's a pulsing in the genital area... and everywhere in my body.

This was a very exciting development, as Sylvia was tapping into the very core of creativity and its orgasmic nature. Using guided imagery, Sylvia became conscious of the sexual polarities of the cosmos and the oscillating of those energies in everything that exists and let herself be regenerated and healed by them.

Many insights flooded into her consciousness concerning her husband, daughter and ways to improve these relationships. She also saw global concerns for the earth's pollution problems that humanity has created and which we must heal to avoid another apocalyptic ride as Noah's and his sons'. That is, assuming God would find humanity worthy of saving again and could find a servant as worthy as Noah to follow the Plan.

At the Crucifixion

For many of us, reading the Bible is a spiritually laden experience, as we turn to various passages to find inspiration and wisdom. When a person regresses to a lifetime wherein he or she lived among those figures of ancient lore, messages contained within the Bible take on a new sense of relevance. For Evelyn, the idea behind a message — and a messenger — was to become an intimately personal one.

At the time of this session, Evelyn reported that since her divorce 13 years earlier, she had not been able to shake off her sense of loss. She knew she needed to go beyond her past to continue to grow, and she wanted to work on the issues that were keeping her stuck. She felt that if she could trace her sense of loss to a past even deeper than this lifetime, she might finally feel a sense of resolution. She regressed to, she said, "*about 2000 years ago, in Jerusalem.*" She was an adolescent male named Ezekiel, wearing sandals and a robe with a sash at the waist.

I'm standing in the marketplace. There's food, pottery, some weapons, swords, shields and shoes. I'm on my way somewhere...

I'm in a room in a house in the town. It's all connected. I'm supposed to pick up a message. There's more than one person. An old man is there and a younger man, a Jesus-figure. Something is in writing. I can't read it. I'm aware of taking it, and feel that it's important, but scary. These people are very sweet and it's sort of surprising at how gentle they are.

Emotions swelled as Evelyn experienced Ezekiel's feelings and began to weep:

> I feel a lot of sadness. I think I know that he's going to die. I think he's a close friend of my family. I've been peripheral. I'm an adolescent boy, but being in his presence. The people around him are special, too. He communicates to me that everything is all right. He's very happy. He's fine. He's not confused or tormented or upset. I feel just incredibly sad that when he leaves he's going to take that special energy of peace and healing with him. But he says no, but I can't relate to that.

Evelyn reviewed what Ezekiel did with the message:

> I think I'm going to take the message back to my parents. Both of my parents are involved. He's telling them that whoever's supposed to come and get him are on their way. They're upset but they know it's true. They understand that they don't have to do anything...

> I'm at the crucifixion, but I don't feel as upset anymore. There are fifty or sixty people who get it - what's going on, and it doesn't feel so bad and the energy is there. I understand that it's still there and what he said was true. He's a very androgynous figure, which I find soothing as an adolescent boy. There's a lot of persuasion in that. I'm on the more feminine side of maleness in that life. Something gets completed in that time for me, a rite of passage. There's a lot of permission for me to go on with my life as it is. I grow up and do whatever studying I had to do. I normally feel a lot of peace that I'm aware other people don't have, and I can definitely trace it back to that experience...

I die an old man in my sleep. It's not dramatic. There's a lot of drama around me, but I don't seem to be in the middle of it much.

After leaving the body of Ezekiel, Evelyn reviewed the purpose of that lifetime and how it relates to her present:

To safely have a powerful spiritual experience, and to witness it through the life that I led. The peace that I experienced was a witnessing. It's okay to be at peace.

I've been taught that life is supposed to be hard, but mainly where I am is expanding into more and more peace ... the idea that you could live in peace and love would be wonderful. There's a lot of healing for me to do, and it's okay for me not to know where I'm going next. Part of the healing for me is to get over needing to know.

The vivid emotions associated with this regression were a powerful confirmation to Evelyn that she could be at peace with herself and her life. The rare quality of spiritual love she felt as a witness to Jesus' enduring energy dissolved her personal disappointment from her failed marriage.

His fear of loss was never manifested, as he remained at peace long after Jesus' death at the cross. Reclaiming that wonderful quality of spiritual fulfillment filled a void that had been missing in Evelyn's marriage. Seeing herself as having once been on the feminine side of maleness and Jesus' presence as androgynous gave Evelyn a deep appreciation of her own wholeness and that as fully enlightened spiritual beings, we transcend the limits of sexual stereotypes.

CHAPTER TWELVE:
AMERICAN HISTORY UP-CLOSE AND PERSONAL

The following three dual-gender stories, while different, let us sample a few slices of American history. Each reviewed a past life during a part of America's development and each review offered these individuals something they needed in order to deal with life in America today.

A Gift He Earned

Most gifted artists, musicians, actors and dancers draw upon their feeling natures, excelling at expressing their right-brain talents, traditionally associated with the 'feminine' side of our being. Roger, a male musician was a female musician in a past life. One may well wonder if an etheric memory cell was stored and carried talent from one lifetime to another and if he developed his current sensitivities as a result of having been a woman so that those sensitivities came more naturally in this life.

Roger was a successful piano teacher and performer but felt his creative juices running dry. He hoped exploring past lives would yield new spiritual insights and inspiration to boost his musical career. With no preconceptions of what his soul records would show, Roger was open-minded to the possibilities. He regressed to a 41-year-old woman in Texas named Elisha, wearing brown wooden sandals, a skirt and a plaid shirt, in 1897, Elisha's situation was desolate:

> Everything is drying up everywhere and all I see is mounds of dirt. There's an Indian village. I have to walk through grass to get to the water, which I have to carry back in a bucket. I bring water all the time. For food, we shoot animals and there is grain and corn.

> It's a nice sunny day, but I feel like there's fear. We have to protect ourselves from the enemy, the Indians.

Everybody is inside the house. I hear a lot of noises and people are crying. I hear gunfire. I see a man with a moustache and hat protecting the house and protecting me. I'm in love with him. There's a close relationship between us. I'd feel terrible if anything happened to him. He doesn't want anybody to hurt us. We're on the Indian's land. Another lady with her child is there. She's my sister. Her husband was killed.

We're safe at this point. We've been here alone, among only a few houses. The Indians don't like us there.

Elisha lived in fear of an ever-present and real threat of confrontation between settlers and Indian Tribes defending their territory, knowing that she and her kin were clearly unwelcome. [*NOTE*: When the first Europeans arrived, what is now known as Texas was home to roughly 30,000 Native Americans living among ten different tribes. In the 1800's, Texas frontier settlers fought to protect their families and homes during raids by Native Americans attempting to slow the settlement of the western part of state.] Thus far in his regression, not much seemed relevant to Roger's present concerns. Progressing ahead, Roger saw:

My man gets shot. I'm 53. We never had our own children. We don't know who shot him. I'm very sad. I have nothing to live for. I felt worthless after my husband died. My sister's son is very grown up. He's taking care of us, doing a lot of work. I feel a great love for him.

As this development was unlikely to yield the inspiration Roger was seeking, he was guided further to review Elisha's childhood family circumstances:

We lived in a big house. I'm 10 years old in our living room. There's a big hallway with flowered wallpaper and there's a piano in the living room. My father plays it. I like to tinker with it. I have a very strict piano teacher who's very stern, not very nice. My lessons are too long and I can't wait for them to be finished.

Having traced his past life roots to a vital link to his present, Roger was asked to continue his review until something else of significance took place:

I'm grown up, but in the same room. I still play and I play well. I like the piano very much now. I play mostly to myself. I'm leaving the house, down the steps, the dirt road, walking by big trees. I'm going to the store to get some things. There's a car accident with an old man. It's not a major accident. I think it's funny. Everybody is friendly and it's a nice town. My father has lots of money. I'm just waiting for the right man to get married.

There's one person that I like. I think people like me just because we have money. My father owns some businesses. I'm very close to my mother. My grandmother still lives in the house. She's very old. I see pavement. I love that house. I don't want to leave that house.

Roger experienced Elisha's unhappiness as a young woman who was attached to her home and family of origin, yet was forced to leave them behind and obediently follow a spouse. Elisha had left circumstances of privilege where she had relied upon her father's money for support, only to rely then upon her husband for protection amidst hostile surroundings. Roger saw the purpose of that life:

To witness the family unit and caring, to share, gain independence and let go of people I loved.

Elisha had not fulfilled that purpose, as she was unable to let go of her husband after he died. Asked how Elisha filled the void left by her husband, Roger said, "I learned to have a love of nature in his place." Perhaps the most revealing insight came when Roger saw how that lifetime related to his present incarnation:

> A person, who has since passed away, gave me the money so I could have the freedom to advance my studies — a benefactor in this lifetime — was my father then. My independence now gives me a lot of strength, to rely on myself rather than others.

Given Elisha's helplessness as a widow in a Texas prairie home, it is easy to understand why maintaining self-reliance is so important to Roger. Upon marrying, Elisha had also left behind her music, as it was apparently considered unimportant by her husband. Yet, the years of early training with a strict piano teacher remained within Roger's soul, since what came only by discipline and effort then, is a natural gift now. Roger's soul had worked hard at learning the piano as a young girl then, which is likely why it came easily to him this time around.

It was especially moving to Roger to see that his benefactor is the same soul as was Elisha's father, her earliest role model and inspiration as a pianist. Roger later confessed that, prior to this session he had been privately struggling to reconcile feelings of unworthiness with feelings of entitlement in receiving his benefactor's largesse. In retrospect, however, Roger could imagine that, had Elisha remained in her hometown community where she could have continued to develop her piano talent, her life would have progressed much differently. In a way, Roger could now see his benefactor's generous gift of financial support as having been earned through his/her suffering in a past lifetime, if not in the present life. When Roger asked for guidance about his present life purpose and his musical career, he saw how the nature of sound impacts more than just the sense of hearing, an important revelation and inspirational conclusion to his session:

The guidance is to be open now because if I don't share my thoughts, I won't be able to grow. Because of my being overly self-protective, I am still so needy. In the present, I've been criticized and mocked for thinking and for being differently from others.

I've had a great need to express what I feel without fear of being criticized. The best vehicle for that is sound. I see how sound affects the body and it's much more important than what we think it is. Sound is not just to be listened to; it's absorbed and felt by the entire body.

There's an incredible ringing in my ears of different pitches. I have to get out of its way and to stop molding it into what I think it should be. I have to relax and allow it to happen.

Civil War Sweethearts

If you have an uncanny affinity to a certain historical period, it may be because you once lived in that period, wherein your soul suffered, grew in joy or learned a vital lesson. Present associations, history books, or television or museum displays of artifacts from that period may stimulate your unconscious memories of it. By reviewing our soul-journeys in past lives, we bring alive the dry facts of history while also deepening our spiritual understanding of ourselves.

Such was the case with Linda, who wanted to investigate her past lives out of her curiosity as to whether, where and when she lived before. Only after her regression did Linda share with me that she had always been fascinated with the period of history to which she regressed, and now understands why.

Linda's review of a former lifetime began with a fourteen-year-old boy named Ben, in the midst of the Civil War. He was wearing a blue uniform that was torn from battle. Because Ben could stand up on the field when the battle was over, he guessed he was probably okay. What transpired next put a very human face on the distant image of a Civil War soldier and is best expressed in Linda's own words, as she saw it all unfold:

> I'm talking to a girl my age about battle. She seems concerned. She's my girlfriend, but he's dressed very nicely, as if she just walked over from her house. She wants to take care of me. I tell her I'm okay. We sit down and talk. She has a father.

> They're wealthy. He's dressed nicely, too. He's coming out of a big building. It's their home. I'm shaken up and she wants to help. When we get there, she wants to make me comfortable. I let her.

> I stay long enough to change clothes and have something to eat. I say good-bye to her, walk back to where the other soldiers are, and wave good-bye. I'm a strong person. I want to go back into battle. ... I'm marching out of that town with troops. The girl is waving and crying. She's afraid I might get hurt. I feel lucky to be able to go and fight again. I have my arm around one of my fellow soldiers, trying to laugh with him.

The young soldier's bravado in being glad to fight the good cause soon disappeared. Linda did not have to go far to reach the end of that life, when she moved ahead in time to Ben's next significant event:

> I was killed in battle with a bayonet through me.

Linda shared the lesson of that lifetime and how that life related to her present:

> That I'm strong and I fight for what I believe in. I'm always crusading for something and usually take action if

I feel strongly about something. I always have had an interest in the Civil War. The girl in the past is my present sister. We care about each other a lot. We're always there to support each other.

Linda later said that seeing herself in the Civil War gave new meaning to her seemingly unrelated interest in that period and helped her understand that what we call coincidence often echoes something more profoundly meaningful. Seeing, too, that her once-soldier soul transcends gender gave Linda the permission she needed to continue fighting for her beliefs, despite others' judgments. This lifted her out of her early self-limiting conditioning, which had been making her feel somehow wrong or embarrassed for holding to, and acting upon, her firm convictions.

Seeing her current sister in the past role of a caring girlfriend deepened Linda's love for her even further. It also reinforced the idea that devotional love is greater than sexual attraction, and must accompany a sexual relationship in order for her to be happy.

Revolutionary War Comrades

All parents hope to be able to provide their children with more than the basic physical necessities of life. We strive to be good role models for them and a source of inspiration and strength to last them through good times and bad. We also hope to instill in them values that will lead them to well-informed judgments in their own lives as adults. Beth asked all this of herself as a parent but was having a hard time fulfilling that desire.

Beth was approaching her middle age years and was concerned about her adult daughter, Jodi, and how best to guide Jodi through her own struggles. Beth had long ago divorced Jodi's father and was openly lesbian. Jodi was also struggling to determine her own sexual preference. Beth knew that Jodi had to make her own decisions, yet Jodi wanted Beth's advice and appreciated her love. Beth felt a deep sense of closeness to Jodi and wondered if they had been together in other lives. Beth regressed easily to a past lifetime when she and Jodi had been together. Both were men in a battlefield scene:

> I see myself in Revolutionary times in the United States. We're between Concord and Lexington in a field of men. Actually, it must be a time in-between battle, because we're just enjoying good spirits rather than harsh gunfire. We're like good buddies. A comradery exists between us. He got killed in that war.

Beth could not hold back tears as she reviewed the above scene and had to pause to compose herself before continuing:

> That was very painful. I was with him. I survived the war. When I went back, a part of myself dies with the tragedy of that war and the loss of this person in my life. For a while, I tried to take care of his wife and family as well as my family. Eventually, a husband came for her and took care of her family.

The purpose of that lifetime and its relationship to Beth's present life was clear to her:

> To learn that it is possible to remain united in spirit, while separated physically. As mother and daughter, we came together in a very powerful physical way in this life, almost too powerful. Once again, we are expanding our beings in relation to each other, to help each other find illumination. I see the kundalini energy being awakened within us both. I am to use it for healing. It's like we're soaring together spiritually.

While Beth and her daughter had been close comrades in war as men, they both had struggled in this life with confusion over their sexual identities. As a man, Beth loved women, yet felt spiritually united with another man. Although now in the body of a woman, Beth maintains her attraction to women and a close spiritual bond with her daughter, carried over from that lifetime as two males.

Another fascinating link between these lives is that both men suffered the evils of war. Perhaps their souls' revulsion toward war and men's base drives for power led them to want to be female in their current lives. Yet, though dwelling in the flesh of the 'softer' sex, their internal programming remained sexually attracted to women.

This perspective gave deeper meaning to Beth's understanding of her own sexual identity and enhanced her love for Jodi even more. Beth's experience served to more fully confirm the real and inextricable interplay between the forces of Spirit, flesh and blood.

CHAPTER THIRTEEN: NATIVE AMERICAN TIMES

In addition to being dual-gender souls the connecting thread among the following three stories is their Native American past lives. Although these cases could have been included within the Dual-Racial chapter, they seemed to belong together apart from other stories. Those who review Native American past lives will forever be more sensitized to the plight of today's Native American descendants.

When Rites Seem Wrong

Nora uncovered through her past life regression a very complex set of puzzle pieces to add to her present life story. Nora was generally discontented at the time of her session, with unsettled feelings about her career, relationships and children. Although married, she was involved with another man and couldn't shake her attachment to him. She was also struggling with her role as stepmother to a child by her husband's first marriage. She hoped her past lives could shed light on her unhappiness and clarify her present life purpose. Nora would require more counseling to resolve her difficulties, but this session gave her a story to ponder that was deeply analogous to her situation.

Nora regressed into a male Native American lifetime in 1806, in Cape Cod, wearing only moccasins and leather hanging straight down over the lower part of his body. As the story unfolded, it was clear that he was on a mission amidst a lot of anger and confusion:

> I'm walking in the woods and there are leaves on the ground. I'm going out to a field to pick some berries and it's a bright day in the fall. I can smell the dampness of the leaves as I walk. There are a lot of trees and the light is diffused. I can feel the sun going in and out of my face as I pass through the branches.

I'm not the chief of the tribe but I am one of the leaders. I'm on some kind of a hunt but not for game. I'm carrying a knife in one hand. The feeling is of stalking something. I'm looking for something but I'm not sure what it is. I keep seeing a baby, but I'm not carrying a baby. A woman in the tribe has the child. She's someone who's been entrusted to me, like an obligation. Somebody died. I don't think the child is mine. My sister died.

Someone older is telling me that I have to take care of this person. The person who's telling me this is not a relative. Someone killed my sister. There's a lot of anger. It's the baby of the person who killed my sister. The murderer was sent away.

Nora moved ahead in time. The next significant event was a very sad development:

I feel like I'm walking away and there's a feeling of leaving something behind. It feels as if I have great big mitts on my hands and I can't move them, they are a heavy weight. It feels as if they're bandaged, but they're not bandaged. I feel immobilized. My right hand feels twisted, as if they're not going the right way. I didn't communicate to anyone before leaving the tribe. Someone else will take care of my obligation. It will be okay. I just keep walking. The feeling in my hands is really strange. They just keep twisting. When I look down, what I see are very lean and agile hands, long skillful fingers, but this twisting feeling is still there, like I can't use them. I can't do the things I want to do. These hands just get in the way, like it's a physical deformity.

I'm leaving because I can't take the place I feel I should take in the tribe or do the things I feel I should be doing. I feel like someone has been taking care of me and I should have been doing the caring. There's a lot of shame. I'm leaving because I don't want that person to take care of me, that woman with the baby.

There's a young, very pretty woman. She's someone I'd like to be with - a member of my tribe. This deformity keeps me from being able to have honor. I don't have the right to claim her. I can't do the things that will entitle me to be with her or make her want to be with me. So, I'm just going to leave.

To learn the source of this deformity, Nora regressed to just before his hands were deformed and described what took place:

Fire comes to mind. I was twelve years old. I see my hands in fire, reaching through the fire to get something. I hear a dull roar, and there's a lot of fire. I don't feel heat, though. My hands feel really cold. I see a really white light...

There's someone older, an old man. It was a test, something to do with clarity and purity. He's watching, knowing that this is really hard, not like he thinks I'm in danger.

There are eyes there in the background. Other boys didn't have to do it. The old man is a teacher. He thinks there's something I'm supposed to do and I don't think I can do it...

I stopped the test and pulled back. It's crazy -1 feel like I don't need this test. There's just no reason for it. That decision makes me stronger; I feel myself growing very tall, and there are people who are afraid of me. It feels like the pulling-back made me stronger, not incapacitated.

But the twisting put a barrier between other people and me.

There should have been an injury or some cross to bear because I pulled back. It made me stronger and set me apart. I have a sense of respect now. There were a lot of people who looked up to me after that and looked to me for answers.

The young woman I loved was his daughter; I couldn't have her because I resisted the old man. I think we were supposed to be together. It was part of this packaged deal, but I can't because I broke away. I was very lonely. I would have preferred to be like everyone else, but I was different.

By rejecting this critical test, he had defied the elder of the tribe and thus the tribe's traditions. Moving to the end of this life, Nora described how things turned out:

I'm old, but keep going. My hands are crippled and my body is frail. After I left the tribe I went somewhere where people didn't know me and I took a background role. I worked the field and didn't do very much. I led a really quiet life. I feel a sadness, but a quiet peace.

Looking back from outside the body after his death, Nora assessed the purpose of that lifetime and how it related to her present:

I'm not sure I learned or succeeded there. I didn't want the role I had. I learned to be with myself I saw a lot of things that other people do, but I don't feel like I was able to give any of that back. I didn't serve as a guide. I was just there to see. I was supposed to be a guide but I didn't fulfill it. I left the people that were important and the things that were familiar. I wasn't willing, so I had to leave all that behind. My will was very strong...

Some things are the same now although my circumstances are different. My current husband was the old man who tested me. There's a lot of pain around that old man. I keep seeing him watching me. There's a feeling that I must follow him now and do things that he says. He's a leader, a wise man and an authority in the group. He has this role with me in particular.

In that life, I resisted the things I was supposed to do because I knew it was wrong to cause that pain. There's a real tug there. I knew the way, but who was I to know the way? The old man was wise and was supposed to know, but I thought he was wrong.

This caused there to be two factions in my tribe and the one respected me because I resisted the old man. The young woman then was the same soul as the other man in my present life. I didn't like that baby.

Nora had a lot to digest. The Indian boy was unfaithful to the old man, to whom he was entrusted. Had he remained faithful to the old man against his own judgment, and not backed away from his rite of passage, he would have earned the old man's daughter. Instead, he sacrificed love and honor within the tribe for the integrity of his own inner voice. This resulted in sadness, loneliness and a *"quiet peace"* which had been painfully absent from Nora's present life.

The issue of obligation was important. Nora saw that she had not fulfilled the past obligation to care for a baby. Now again, she was expected to care for another's child, her husband's child by his first wife. To honor the obligations of her soul, Nora felt she must stay and care for this child because she felt a powerful maternal calling.

Nora's current dilemma resonated deeply with her past. Fire symbolizes human passion and Nora was engulfed again, immobilized and weighed down, as if her hands were tied. Two dual-gender associations link Nora's past with her present: the woman he then loved could not defy her father and leave the tribe with the boy, even if it was her heart's desire. The soul that was the young woman then, to whose love the Indian had not *"earned the right"*, is now the *other man*, loving Nora now in defiance of what is *right* by the social standards of today. Remaining faithful to her husband means she cannot have that other man, her conflicts again pitting honor and duty against emotions to challenge Nora again, to follow a course true to her soul.

Nora's story brings to mind the similarity between the difficult process of a baby's physical birth and the equally difficult process of a soul's spiritual birth. Both can force us to get through a fine mess before beginning a new life.

Trapped By Indecision

If you have ever felt trapped by circumstances, you may relate to Debra's dilemma and the hopeful idea that what is lost to you in one lifetime may return in another. Debra was discontent in her marriage. She and her husband had been growing steadily apart, seeming to have little in common besides family and household concerns. He was a good provider for Debra and their daughter, but she questioned whether that was enough to sustain a marriage. Debra loved her husband and was saddened by the emotional and spiritual distance between them. She did not want to blame her husband for her unhappiness, but felt trapped in a situation that was draining her zest for life.

Believing in reincarnation and sensing that she knew her present husband and her daughter with whom she was very close, in a former life, Debra wondered if seeing how and where, through past life regression, could help her overcome her timidity and become more assertive in her marriage. Debra regressed to see herself as a ten-year-old Native American boy wearing moccasins on his feet and leather or suede material for pants and a jacket:

> I'm peaceful as a youth. I'm balancing myself on two stones over a brook or some kind of stream. I have a net in the water and I'm fast. I can catch them with my hands sometimes. There's ways we block part of the stream and catch the fish going down. Mother cooked them over the fire. She's proud of me, I can tell. I'm the oldest son and I have a sister who's five years younger. I'm protective of her. My Father is a good teacher and he is one of the respected men in the tribe. He will be one of the members of the council.

Moving ahead in time to the next significant event, the young brave's tribe was at war with another tribe:

> We're on horseback with about 20 young braves; I have a spear in my hand. We're going to attack another tribe that has moved in too close to our hunting area. We're going through the village. I care only about the leaders of that tribe. If we can eliminate the leaders, then the tribe will move on. There are a lot of children and women screaming and running. It's an easy victory.

Some time after this victory, a marriage ceremony rich with custom and symbolism took place:

> There's a woman in the tribe and she seems interested in me. I'm concerned for my little sister because she wants to marry my best friend. That's good. I marry by my choice.

> At her wedding ceremony, I have mixed feelings. I can tell she's happy, smiling, but I'm more of a warrior. I want children. I don't have much feeling for the woman

that I will marry. One of the elders marries us. As preparation before the ceremony, I spend time alone and she does the same. The ceremony is simple. We exchange gifts, something that's handmade. She gives me a blanket for my horse and I made a necklace for her with claws and things from my hunting.

The tribe did not remain at peace. Once again, the issue of territory rights came to a boil:

Our village is in trouble. There's anger among young braves over the land and the government. They want to fight. I'm angry. I see a council of the elders trying to calm down the younger braves who want to fight. They sense our destiny and know it's not the right way.

Debra next described a period of turmoil for the tribe when he was twenty-seven:

I am a hunter and I work with the tribe, the Iroquois Nation. I am one of the leaders of the younger braves. I'm known for my hunting abilities. I'm near a mountain range. I see deer, rabbits and fish in streams. One of the men of peace has died and there's much division within the tribe. There's some letter following what the elders said about trying to keep the peace. Others were war-like. I'm leaning more towards the warrior but I'm very confused. I'm in a wooded area on a trail; it's in the fall in the upper New York area, about 1802. I have to be alone to think. I go to a place that's high in the mountains and I've been there for a while asking for guidance. I'm asking why have I been such a good warrior; if I was born with these kinds of skills, why shouldn't I fight? Something inside me says it's wrong; there's a lot of turmoil and sadness ahead.

Fifteen years passed until his death:

> I'm on the ground and it's snowing. I've been wounded.
> A man is standing above me dressed in furs, a trapper.
> I'm in my early 40's. He's going to kill me. I'm looking
> over all of the land. It's so peaceful, so beautiful, like I
> had never noticed before. I feel like I'm reviewing
> everything, because where I'm looking is where I grew
> up. There was so much anger and the hostility between
> tribes seemed so wasted.

The purpose of that lifetime held great meaning to Debra as she
evaluated what her soul was meant to learn and how it applies to
her present lifetime:

> I should have channeled the anger. I developed my skills
> to the point where I should have used them to survive
> rather than to kill. I had a choice between peace and war.
> I needed to learn humility. I died from a white man
> instead of in battle. It was not a noble way to die. He
> caught me by surprise, alone.

> My present husband was the trapper in that life and he
> now mirrors a lot of the anger I had. I have to learn to
> listen to guidance and go the way of peace, to show him.
> It's not so much that he took my life but the way he did it.
> There's no hatred, because it brought me peace and ended
> my problems within my existence. He took away my
> chance to decide and now he has to give me the freedom
> to make choices. He's supposed to let me be free now.
> My sister then is my little girl today. She's very good.

Reviewing a past life in which she was a male hunter/warrior
renewed Debra's courage to assert her right to make her own
decisions. Debra now sees that her own indecisiveness is a bigger
trap than anything else and that if she wants her husband to

respect her, she must respect her own wants, needs and rights. Debra's love for her past-life sister, their present daughter, was another link between past and present. It gave Debra reason to forgive her trapper-now-husband for severing that past tie, as he restored it in the present by being a responsible father to that same soul.

Realizing that by providing for her physical needs in the present her husband was doing his best to compensate for taking her life in the past, Debra gained new compassion and respect for him. It also became clear that her marriage was not impeding her growth, but actually provided a firm base of support from which she was free to grow as much as she desired.

A Medicine Man and His Mother's Gift

Once we begin to explore our past lives, it is natural to wonder how many we have had and if we can ever review them all, making fully conscious our previously unconscious storehouse of soul memories. Gina had successfully reviewed several lifetimes over the course of many sessions and several years. Her ongoing interest in this work was to complete her karma and live a more fully spiritually awakened present.

Gina reconnected with past life Native American roots that held deep meaning for her. This was not her only review of a male past lifetime, but it was unusually rich with detail, which adds authenticity to her experience. It is retold here in its entirety, as Gina saw it:

> I'm a barefoot boy in a Native American tribe. It's time for me to go to sleep and I ask my Mama to tell me one last story before I go to sleep. Mama leans down near my bed of straw on the floor of our hut and stroked her hand a few inches above my chest and head, and then she closes her eyes and lays her hands beneath by head, giving me some gentle support. She looks at me and smiles and motions for me to be quiet, and then she closes her eyes

again and sees the Great White Light with us. She is awed and quiet before the Great White Light that speaks to her in many tongues and shows her pictures to tell the people.

But, tonight, the White Light gives her no pictures, but she gives me these words: "Peace, be still at heart, and know that all is good." She kisses me above my eyes in the center of my forehead and then rises and quietly walks out of our tent. Immediately, my spirit joined the Great White Light and I am at peace for the rest of the night...

It's the next morning and it's the big hunt. Papa goes with the other men of our village to search out a big cat and maybe a deer or two. They had sharpened all their arrows to give them pointed spearheads. It was important that the spearheads were as sharp and long as they could be, so that there would be no mistake when it hit, that it would penetrate deeply into the beast. I had watched them make their arrows in the village. It always frightened me. I didn't like the taste of meat, somehow. It seemed too tough to eat.

I was a very shy boy and I didn't talk very much. I liked to watch the beautiful fire that would keep us warm and give us light at night and teach us many things about the Great White Light, the Spirit moving us, burning and consuming all life. And I especially love sitting by the fire as Mama tells stories to the people. One at a time Mama would go around the circle and say the names of everyone present. As she spoke their names she would close her eyes and see the story in her mind. Sometimes the story was only two words long and sometimes the story would be many words and gestures but each story was a message from the Great White Light. Our people knew that and Mama was very special to them.

When I awake the next morning, the men are gone for their hunt. Mama is building the fire for the day and just getting the sticks together for the nighttime, when the men will return with their prize, hungry and cold. After she builds the fire, she goes into the tent and sits in silence for a long time. I look for my friend, the little girl who lives three tents away from me. This is washday and we carry her wash and our wash and many of our neighbors' wash many miles away to the stream that flows through nearby hills past three Indian villages. We all share that stream. We also carry two buckets to bring water back and I have two buckets over my shoulders, made out of hollowed-out tree trunks. I had helped to carve them and make them sturdy. Each bucket has a hole on either side with wound ferns making a rope to hold the bucket and a long, sturdy branch goes behind my neck across both shoulders to support both buckets. On each end of the branch are deep grooves where the rope handles hangs. We are walking very quickly down to the water. We want to finish our tasks a soon as we can. When we return to the village it is almost dark. The Sun is slowly sinking to the west and some birds of prey are above the forest line, indicating that dead flesh was being brought our way.

We know that the hunt is over, yet the wind speaks to us of ill news. We are starting to get very cold as we wait, so the Medicine Man comes out to be with us. He lit the fire and starts to sing a long, low chant as he sways back and forward on his knees with his fists clenched together, one above the other, as if he is stirring some invisible brew. He is invoking the forces of good to be with us. Mama is still in her tent, quietly waiting for the men to return. I run into the tent to be with her and rest my head on her lap. She motions for me to be quiet and lays her hands on my head. I know that we are going to be alone together for a long time now.

When the men return, they are carrying a big cat and Papa. Both are bleeding badly and both are without Spirit. My heart is very heavy. Mama cries to herself and sobs deeply at her loss. I am very angry that the White Light let Papa be hurt so badly. And then, I understand that the cat had claws, and that she was protecting her mate when she plunged forward at Papa. And now both the cat and Papa were at rest. That night no food is eaten.

Both the cat and papa are offered to the gods so that we might have peace once more in our village and with the big cats. All through the dark night, the men of the village do a solemn dance, moving in constant small steps, weaving back and forth around the great campfire, letting Papa know that we are in sorrow at his unexpected departure.

The women of the village stay inside their tents with their children, except for Mama and me. Mama dips her hands into the bowels of the cat and tears away its liver from inside and throws it into the fire. This makes blue flames rise high in the center of our circle. We watch the fire burn while chanting the burial chant, asking the Great White Light to protect our tribe. As the fire starts to burn down, the men sit on the ground with their legs folded and pass a long thin pipe into which had been put the delicate seeds of the poppy flower which was ground to a fine powder around the great circle. Ordinarily, I would not be present at such a passing of the pipe, as no women or children participate in the pipe passing. But tonight the Medicine Man takes Mama and me with him on either side of him in the circle and asks that our Spirits be strengthened and fortified by the Great White Light and that we should continue to find joy, health and strength in the community of the tribe. From one to next, the pipe passes until the Sun shines above the horizon. That signals the time for us to rise from the circle and to know that Papa is free from the flesh, to rise in Spirit, with our blessings and our love.

From that time on, I stay close by to Mama. While all of the other boys my age prepare for the Indian initiation rites, I am afraid of the hunt and of the blood that might be shed in the fight with the cats who were hungry for prey. Mama worries for me. She prays to the Great White Light each day and night to be given the courage to send me away when the time comes. One night, she has a vision as she sits by my side with her legs and arms crossed as I sleep in the tent. She watches carefully as my spirit rises high above my body in tall, clear form and speaks to her, using her spirit name. The message is that she must not worry any longer, for I am destined to train with the Medicine Man to become wise in the ways of healing and protection for the tribe. Her heart fills to the brim with love for me; at last she can rest.

The next day, Mama and I walk to the Medicine Man's tent and wait outside for him to appear and sit sternly in front of his tent as he usually does. Mama tells him about her vision and asks the Medicine Man to take me with him and teach me his art. The Medicine Man looks deep and long into my eyes until I feel my chest begin to swell with a burning sensation. He turns to Mama and nods, then, lifting his head to face the heavens, he holds his arms out wide and sings a prayer to the gods for a sign to see if I will be able to withstand the initiation test for this difficult calling. The Medicine Man brings me into his teepee and motions to Mama that she should leave.

Without any warning, my insides begin to scream in pain and the air seems to fill my lungs with a horrible smell. My knees cannot support me and my stomach begins to cramp severely. My skin cries out in a sweat, as my body burns hotter than I had ever known possible. The Medicine Man is calm and peaceful. He helps me to a section of his teepee that is very dark and isolated, where I lay, afraid and confused, not knowing what is taking place in my body. I had never been this ill before.

He leaves me alone with my fever as the darkness comes. Still the fever burns within me. I have never known such torture; just when I think that surely I will die, I look up to find my friend sneaking inside the teepee. She sensed that I was in need and wanted to be with me. I take her hand and squeeze it very hard and ask her to please go to scrape some fresh, hard bark from the Litchi nut tree and bring it to me in a bowl of boiling water with a cloth. When she returns with the medicine, I ask her to rub the hot damp cloth on the soles of my feet and then I drink what was left of the red bark tea. Lest she be scolded for being in the Medicine Man's teepee, she quickly runs away when she is through and leaves me once again alone.

When morning came, my fever disappeared and I felt new life filling my veins. The Medicine Man helped me to sit up and placed a string of sacred beads around my neck and said a solemn blessing over my body. He then cut my finger with a very sharp tool and mixed my blood with his, finger to finger. He said, "He who can heal himself from death's long arm is a brave and mighty warrior of peace. This man shall serve the Gods well by healing others of their pains." Now I understood that the Gods had given me my illness as the sign the Medicine Man sought.

For the next three years, I am a humble servant and an obedient student of the Medicine Man. He demands much, including fasting often for several days at a time while learning about the sacred ritual dances and prayers.

No women are allowed to be near me, not even my mother or my friend, since I am learning how to rely fully upon the Gods for my strength and guidance. I am forbidden from being soothed by the tender touch or the loving voice of a female. Becoming a Medicine Man also means that I am to sacrifice the privilege of taking a bride, so that I will not be bound by the needs of having my own family.

When my training years are passed, the Medicine Man announces to the members of the tribe that I am ready to serve the needs of my people. Together we pray before the tribe for good days ahead and then I leave the circle to seek out Mama. She had aged a great deal in the three years of my absence. She is sitting still and quietly in her tent with her head leaning back against the center post. She looks at me when I enter and smiles. I know that she is very proud to see her son become an honored member of the tribe. As she closes her eyes, I realize that her spirit is preparing to pass into the invisible world. I shut my eyes and watch as her spirit begins to rise. The spirit of Papa stands before her, holding his hand out to her to come with him. He is waiting for her in the light. I inwardly ask, "Mama, tell me one last story before you go to sleep.

She did and it was a beautiful story about a young Medicine Man who lives a long life with the people of his tribe. He has a wonderful helpmate, a woman friend, who shares his work. He has also been given a precious gift from his mother, the ability to see the Great White Light and to speak its truths to the people in the form of stories. At that, she cuts the invisible cord that had kept her attached to her earthly body and waves goodbye.

After a, moment, I stand up and turn to leave the tent. The whole tribe is gathered in a large circle to hear what news I have to bring them. I breathe a very deep breath and call out to all that we have cause for a joyous celebration that Mama has joined her husband and is very happy. I tell them of the gift that Mama has given me for the tribe, her great inner vision, so that our people will always have the wisdom of the Great White Light to tell them stories.

For three days and nights, there are ceremonial dances and chanting with much to eat and drink for every man, woman and child. It is our farewell celebration of Mama's great and prosperous journey homeward and of her happy reunion with Papa.

Gina was given important guidance when she asked how that lifetime's purpose related to her present:

It was to understand the reality of the invisible Spirit world and my own potential as a healer. My mother then is a close female friend today and the Medicine Man is my present spiritual teacher. The female friend from that lifetime is another female friend now.

I need to trust in the gifts that I've been given and have been well-prepared to use in my present life, to be a channel for healing again.

Gina had enjoyed good relationships with men in the present and was pleased to know that she herself had once been the kind of man that she most sought and admired in the present. This was not the only Native American lifetime she reviewed, but it was the most peaceful, and the guiding *"Great White Light"* was the same as she often experienced in her meditations.

Gina's review of that past life was occasionally interrupted by tearful pauses as its sublime beauty and compassion filled her with awe and reinforced for her the message that she is as worthy and loved in the present as she was in the past. Gina now offers a range of modalities to others as an alternative therapist with a deeper appreciation for her own instincts and intuitions.

Another connection between Gina's Medicine Man life and her present is that now she is devoted to her marriage and to raising their two children. This was a commitment she had to forego as a Medicine Man, but is now glad to have. Although it takes time away from other pursuits, she wouldn't give it up for the world. Knowing that one can just as easily fall into the trap of becoming too spiritually ambitious as being too ambitious about worldly achievement, Gina now strives for balance in her life, rather than forsaking the physical for the spiritual.

CHAPTER FOURTEEN: THE FABRIC OF COMMUNITY

Sometimes we forget that no man or woman is an island. The two dual-gender stories in this chapter also remind us of that truth.

Love Transcends the Odds

So ingrained are our fears of being judged by others, that we too often make decisions based on those fears as we tell ourselves *"real women don't..."* or *"real men don't..."* These fears, as Faith learned through past life regression, transcend gender but not human nature.

Faith found herself in a surprising love affair with Keith, who was unlike anyone she'd ever known. Their problem was that they came from vastly different cultural/religious backgrounds, which posed a difficult obstacle to them being accepted by their respective communities. Yet, being so comfortable with Keith made Faith wonder if they knew each other in a past life. Faith regressed to see herself as a man in Lebanon, wearing sandals, pants and top that was something like a blouse in the 1600s. Instantly recognizing Keith's soul in that lifetime, Faith continued to call him Keith, although he must have had a different name in that lifetime:

> I see flat tents. Inside my tent is a big, square, flat meeting table. Keith is there; I don't see anyone else. We're co-workers and we have to make a military or government decision but it feels okay. Keith is about ten years older, but it's a close relationship, almost to the point of being homosexual. And then he meets a woman and takes off...
>
> After that, we see each other occasionally, but it's not the same. That period passed and we're no longer co-workers. We're still friendly, but distant. I don't have any other relationships. I see myself doing some real estate business

and I'm all dressed up in a suit jacket. I'm 72 years old when I just pass out of my body peacefully.

The purpose of that lifetime, and its relationship to her present resonated strongly for her:

> I helped a lot of people learn compassion. There are still barriers for us but they can be worked out. They're easier now. Perhaps we are meant to be co-workers again.

The tension within Faith's past-life relationship with Keith came from their past discomfort at being so close emotionally, yet being the same sex and thus afraid of others' perception of their relationship. Allowing that fear to drive them apart hurt not only Faith and Keith, it ultimately also hurt the very community whose judgments they feared. The wise decisions they would have made together because of their love for each other would have benefited their community. Their combined excellent leadership skills were a wonderful asset that became lost to their community once their relationship dissolved.

As that taboo no longer exists, they can now freely explore their feelings for each other as intimate sexual partners without fear of social rejection, but much more is at stake. Their now-different cultural backgrounds create other, non-sexual, obstacles within their respective communities. The common thread in both lives is to need to cope with fears of being judged by others. Then those fears separated them and caused the end of a deep friendship and great source of joy. In her present, Faith intends to rise above the fears of prejudice and trust that her love for Keith can extend to love for their respective communities, which need their combined skills as much as Faith and Keith need each other's companionship and love.

A Tibetan Traveler

Sometimes life challenges are like great mountains to be climbed, figuratively speaking, and we must face trying times alone to get to the top. For Teresa, her present life challenges seemed enormous and she discovered through her past life regression that she was up to the task.

Teresa was in a transition period and hoped that seeing a past lifetime would help to clarify her life purpose. She had been living a somewhat nomadic existence, moving from place to place and not feeling at home in any community. She was a single parent to a healthy and intelligent boy who seemed understandably estranged from others. This worried Teresa as she realized her son needed to belong to a caring community where he could form strong bonds with good adult role models.

Teresa's review of her past life began as a forty-year-old *"very brown"* Tibetan man named Karim in the year 1203. Karim's hair was covered and he was wearing sandals and a robe made of white shiny fabric with long sleeves:

> I have no family and I travel a lot. I see mountains in the distance. I really enjoy the air and the sky in the mountains. I go to the mountains to bring things to people that they are very pleased to receive. I'm not by myself but I am leading animals that are carrying goods. People are expecting me and I have books and something with a lot of color, like stones or cloth with metallic-like thread in it. I have no family. I enjoy the traveling. It's good to find people to be with... Now, instead of mountain villages, I am coming to tent-like places. It seems like a monastery in the mountains and I've left behind the animals and people that followed me. There are a lot of steps that go up to the building.
>
> The sky is still, very blue - always sunny. I've been there before and all this time, I see a smile on my face.

> There are people that greet me as if I'm expected and I stay there. It feels as though it's a home and there's a child there. The child is a young boy that is being cared for there and we have some kind of tie. It's my adopted school age son that I brought there. I stay through the late fall and winter and only travel again when the weather is warm. I am taking things from this place.

Directing Teresa to move ahead to see how things developed, she reviewed Karim's later years:

> I'm in a more permanent place now, sitting inside in a room with a garden in the middle and a fountain. The child has grown and we're talking with books around.

Moving to the end of that life, Teresa described the peaceful scene as death approached:

> I have a grayish beard. I'm ninety. I'm walking with a staff, bent a bit. I've grown weak in that place. I laid down there. There is no surprise. Many people stop and look as if I just fell asleep.

When reviewing the purpose of that lifetime and how it relates to her present she said:

> This man had conviction and he followed a certain belief, going toward things as though he didn't question them. The smile and the sun felt very good. I need to remember that feeling of the sun and the smile, and his conviction.

Teresa saw many parallels between herself and the Tibetan traveler she had been. The appeal of climbing mountains and a monastic environment were both strong for her, as well as her commitment to raising her son to the best of her ability.

Seeing how well things went for Karim as a single man strengthened Teresa's confidence in her ability to go on as a single woman, without feeling guilty or incomplete for not having a partner.

Teresa and her son eventually joined a mountainous village communal living situation where they were warmly welcomed among people who not only needed them but also had much to offer them.

CHAPTER FIFTEEN: MORE DUAL-GENDER STORIES BY CONTRIBUTORS:

Dr. Bruce Goldberg: A renowned dentist turned hypno-therapist, Dr. Goldberg has conducted over 33,000 past life regressions on over 11,000 patients and maintains a thriving practice in Los Angeles, CA. He has appeared on CBS news, Oprah, Donahue, Sally Jesse Raphael, Tom Snyder, Jerry Springer, Live with Regis and Kathy Lee, Leeza and numerous other TV and radio shows, has been featured in Time, Omni, Los Angeles Times and the Washington Post. Dr. Goldberg is a member of the Academy of Psychosomatic Medicine, the American Psychological Society, the American Association of Applied and Preventive Psychology and the International Hypnosis Hall of Fame. He is a Past President of the Los Angeles Academy of Clinical Hypnosis and the Mid-Atlantic Hypnotists Examining Council. Dr. Goldberg authored the international best seller Past Lives-Future Lives and The Search for Grace: A documented Case of Murder and Reincarnation, which was made into a CBS movie. His newest book, Soul Healing (Llewellyn, ISBN1-56718-317-4), won the Small Press Association's top metaphysical and spiritual award for 1997.

Phyllis Nelson Grau, MA: Phyllis Nelson Grau lives in Olean, NY, and has been an annual Presenter of esoteric subjects at the International Forum on New Science, since 1991. Phyllis learned spirit de-possession before studying more ordinary hypnotherapy techniques, in 1992. Phyllis earned undergraduate and graduate (MA) degrees from Hunter College, City University of New York, and did Doctoral level studies at State University of New York at Albany. Her broad teaching background includes secondary and college and graduate level courses at several NY schools, colleges and universities. In addition to being a Past Life Therapist, she is a Staff Development Specialist for the NY State Education Dept, serving as a Teacher Center Director.

Rev. Susan Lukegord: Sue Lukegord, (1939-1998), was the founder and director of Sacred Light Center for Esoteric Studies, was a professional Astrologer, Past Life Therapist, healer, lecturer and teacher and since the late 1960s. She earned her Social Services degree in human development from University of Massachusetts and was a legally ordained Minister in the Church of the Living Word. Sue worked with Reverend Paul L. Higgins in Spiritual Frontiers Fellowship and Rockport Colony for many years, leading meetings, spiritual retreats and tours and taught at Bunker Hill Community College in Charlestown, MA. Sue worked by attuning to a person's spiritual essence and bringing forth experiences from past lives, clearing channels for new creative, healing energy. By drawing on her psychic gifts and training in psychology, comparative religion and social work. Sue assisted thousands of seekers in finding practical and spiritual answers to life questions. Sue shared two fascinating stories with this author in a recorded interview just months before her passing.

Rabbi Yonassan Gershom: Rabbi Gershom is a member of the Breslover Hasidic community. He is a well-known storyteller, teacher and writer. He resides in Minnesota and has traveled extensively throughout the USA and abroad. Rabbi Gershom's work on traditional Jewish spirituality and beliefs has appeared in many periodicals and anthologies. He is also the author of Beyond the Ashes: Cases of Reincarnation from the Holocaust. From Ashes to Healing: Mystical Encounters with the Holocaust, and 49 Gates of Light. His newest book is Jewish Reincarnation Stories, which contains the tale from the classical sixteenth-century Hebrew text, Shivchei Ha-Ari that he shares in this chapter.

A Past-Life Treatment of Male Homosexuality
By Dr. Bruce Goldberg

"Although my research shows that approximately 75% of our lives are lived as the same sex, we must change sex in order to grow spiritually." Bruce Goldberg, Soul Healing, Llewellyn

Dr. Goldberg presents this case of a dual-gender soul in his own words, of a male client who saw two lives as a woman. Following the regression details is this author's commentary about the case as it reflects many dual-gender soul issues.

A male homosexual came to my office with the desire to eliminate his previous sexual behavioral patterns. During a past life in ancient Rome he was a female prostitute who very much enjoyed her work of sexually satisfying men.

In another past life in England during the early 1800s, this male patient was again a female, this time a shopkeeper's wife. This was a hard life and her husband was a cruel man who was selfish in bed and physically abused his wife. Having sex with him was more of "doing her duty." The only solace she had in life was a lesbian relationship with a neighbor. In this life she learned the pleasures of homosexual love, whereas her heterosexual relationship was completely unsatisfying.

Within two months following therapy, this male patient broke up with his male lover and has since become engaged to a woman. Two years after this case was completed, a follow-up conversation with this patient revealed that he is very happy with his heterosexual relationship and has had no relapses.

Author's Commentary

This case is a wonderful example of past life therapy's potential to resolve conflicts about sexuality. It is important to recognize that Dr. Goldberg did not advocate that his male patient abandon being a practicing homosexual; the patient's own desire was to alter his sexual behavior pattern.

By exploring two past lives as a woman. Dr. Goldberg's patient likely gained several valuable insights about himself with regard to his feelings toward both men and women. Even beyond the issue of sexual preference and gender identity, this case has much to teach us about a soul's desire to experience and advance through various social structures, which was the unspoken subtext to this man's story.

It is safe to assume that the prostitute's ability to satisfy men sexually, while psychologically empowering to her, was associated with belonging to a taboo social class. By contrast, the English shopkeeper's wife, while likely enjoying the comforts and stature of belonging to a social class of greater prestige, was psychologically powerless in an unhappy marriage to an abusive man. To meet her sexual needs, she became engaged in a lesbian affair, embracing another kind of social taboo.

It would appear that this soul had become well skilled in the use of sex as the currency of relationships, along with gaining understanding that women in any social class, be they prostitute or housewife, are historically less powerful than men. This reiterates what is well known, that social power belongs to men. By taking on a male body, this soul may have reasonably expected to continue climbing the ladder of social status that being male guaranteed.

Because this soul had a pattern of living out sexual taboos, it is no surprise that he would, as a man, first adopt a homosexual lifestyle, for which men in our culture have historically suffered social discrimination! Given this soul's steady social progression from underclass (prostitute) to middle class (shopkeeper's wife), it is also logical that he would want to attain the more coveted, respected status of male head-of-household which, of course, required forming a heterosexual bond. Ironically, despite this soul's experiences that women have less power than men, only by winning the heart and hand of a woman in this life could he achieve the social bearing it would seem his soul desired! The true test of growth for this dual-gender soul in his present lifetime is to become the kind of man whom he, as a former she, may have loved and respected. As a former prostitute and abused housewife his soul surely knows which pitfalls to avoid!

Restoring the Reproductive Web
By Phyllis Nelson Grau, MA

Speaking of dual-gender souls and her work, Phyllis said, "Few people understand that we change genders from one life to another. I find that people keep going around with each other in different lifetimes and whole groups of people are reincarnating together." Phyllis shared this case study about Jack, a thirty-two-year-old whose primary reason for seeking counseling was a difficult relationship with his mother. He hoped to better understand it by reviewing his past lives.

In his past life, Jack was Trudy, an orphan of sorts whose father had died. She and her mother were taken into the household of the mother's brother-in-law. At that time period, females were not considered competent to run their own lives and widows and orphans were sent to live with their nearest male relative.

Thus, Trudy's uncle became her guardian, and he fancied Trudy's mother, his sister-in-law. She was able to keep him at a distance for four years, but eventually had to endure his forced attentions, as there was no place else to go. She became pregnant. The mother was deeply ashamed of her situation and she died due to complications of the pregnancy. This caused rumors in the town, which made it impossible for the uncle to find a proper suitor for Trudy when she was old enough.

Actually this uncle controlled the potential suitors and didn't approve of any of them. He controlled Trudy's inheritance from her father and as long as she didn't marry, then he could continue to control the money. Eventually Trudy replaced her mother in her uncle's bed and used herbal contraceptives and abortifacents supplied by a dear friend who was a midwife. Trudy never did marry and became an old maid in her uncle's house; in effect, being kept as his sex slave!

Seeing that Trudy's uncle was now Jack's mother was quite a shock to Jack! This regression revealed new information that pertained to two of Jack's other problems. First, Jack had a voice problem; he couldn't speak up in a decisive and resonant masculine tone. In effect, this was a throat chakra blockage. We discovered that Trudy had worn a black ribbon with an ivory carving of her mother on it as a choker around her neck to remind her of her mother. The energy of the choker in the former life was restricting Jack's present voice. Jack couldn't speak up to his mother or to anybody else. His voice always sounded weak and compliant, like the voice Trudy used with her abusive uncle.

Another of Jack's present problems related to that lifetime. Trudy had vowed not bear children for her uncle. While Jack had no children in the present, his live-together girlfriend whom he later married had become pregnant several times by him yet miscarried during each first trimester. Because she'd had a prior successful pregnancy in a previous relationship, she knew she was able to conceive and carry a child, so the cause of these miscarriages was a mystery. The past life regression revealed to Jack that if he were to have children, he would be making them for his prior-life uncle who would be, in this life, his children's grandmother!   Jack's wife miscarried at the same time in the pregnancy as when Trudy used the herbal abortifacents.

As therapy, I asked for the appropriate celestial healers to remove the energy of the black ribbon choker and to rebalance the energy of the entire energy field regarding sexuality, creativity and the throat chakra (one of seven energy centers in the etheric body). Jack had throat problems from other lifetimes, and this healing was only the beginning of a lot of other work on his throat area.

Acting on his new insights, Jack went home and talked to his wife about having a baby. After she said YES, he came back and asked to have the vow of NO CHILDREN removed. At his next hypnotherapy session a week later, his High Self was asked to take this restrictive program out of his energy field. This was done and energy was restored to the reproductive web (the term that the High Self used) in the masculine and feminine energy fields. Jack's wife got pregnant ten months later and gave birth to a healthy baby girl to whom Jack is a very attentive father.

Author's Commentary:

When I asked Phyllis if they had seen whether or not Trudy's mother had come back as Jack's present wife, thus continuing the triangle of relationships, she said Jack identified his past-life mother as a different woman he knew in this life. He was also sure his present wife was not connected with that particular past life.

This case demonstrates how two dual-gender souls can be bound together lifetime after lifetime, first in the roles of niece and uncle, then switching sexes to continue their relationship now as son and mother. Phyllis stated that Jack was better able to accept his mother after seeing the details of his past life as

"Trudy" with her then-uncle. Given this background of experience, Jack's mother's undeveloped maternal instinct is easily understood.

Two Cases: *"Homosexuality and Transexuality"*

Interview with Reverend Sue Lukegord:
September 4, 1997, Gloucester, Massachusetts

Sue shared a wealth of experience and wisdom in a free-flowing interview discussion on the topic of Dual-Gender souls, presented herein. She penetrated many core truths about gender identity, the invisible anima and animus within us.

Sue spoke of her start in this work in "the old Baba days" when her heart and throat chakras were opened at a two-day intensive spiritual retreat. After that, she started doing a lot of Akashic Record readings in New York, throughout the United States, Hawaii, Great Britain and the Holy Land, often clearing people of addictions:

SUE: I would purify and seal the room in special way that I was given, and say this Opening to the Akashic Record: I ask God to surround so-and-so and myself in pure white Christ light, so that only love, joy and truth exists between us and the universe. I ask to be lifted in three concentric spheres of light to the Plane of Communication of the Masters who are one heart, mind and will of God. And I ask the Masters, Teachers, loved ones and guides of so-and-so to channel through me now, and I ask the Lords of the Akashic Records to open the records of so-and-so and channel through me now.

"Then, I would monologue [share intuitive insights with the client], and anything that I said, felt or experienced, pertained to the person. I didn't try to review one sex and then another but it seemed to turn out that way, that I would do the same-sex lifetimes, then the other-sex lifetimes. The thing that was immediately striking was that the opposite sex lifetimes resembled the boyfriends and husbands of the women. For the men, they resembled their wives, girlfriends and mothers, and in a definitive way, the males confirmed their female incarnations, saying that they were exactly like some female that was very close to them, most often their wives, but sometimes the mother.

"The females would affirm that the male incarnations were just like their present husbands. One woman, in her male incarnation, was a riverboat gambler and deceiver, who was loose with money. He married but left the wife and children at home and fooled around and was really bad with the money. All he cared about was traveling around, card games and gambling.

This was exactly like this woman's first husband. She is not at all like this in this lifetime, yet she tended to attract this type of man, not just the first spouse, but also almost any man to whom she might be attracted was like this.

So, it seemed to affirm Jung's idea about the anima and animus; that within a man is a female that can be very, very different from the male. Often, they were extremely different. I never found any that were really that much alike."

AMY: What you are saying ties so many threads together, because you've opened the records of the soul to see that we, indeed, meet ourselves as we once were through the opposite sex, which Issie [Isabel Hickey] said over and over again. We are facing our karmic consequences through our relationships.

SUE: There was never a case in which the woman didn't recognize her past life as a male as being like someone she knew in the present. It was always someone very close to them, such as her husband, lover or potential mate.

AMY: So, our past lives dictate the present; we draw to ourselves the exact kind of people we once were. And, our partners really are the projections of how we once were, perhaps the opposite of our current selves.

SUE: That's right, and they may have many other qualities that we ignore, but the thing we're most aware of, and like or dislike, pulls us into a relationship. The wives of the gambling husbands always wanted them to come home. When they stop being resentful stop projecting everything and realize that they're dealing with aspects of themselves, that's when the big transformation takes place. And it is in that sex change relationship that this happens.

I do want to speak about two examples, one of homosexuality and one of transexuality, because these stand out in my mind so much. One day a mother brought her grown son to me. He was homosexual and she hoped that he would understand something or get help from me with his homosexuality. Whether he wanted to come or not, he was very docile when he came.

Reviewing his soul records, his was the first case I had encountered of a soul who refused to take female lifetimes. Only one female lifetime came to the surface, in which she had been poor, abused by her husband, had many children and lived in total misery. After that, he would never take a female lifetime again. He'd had such a bad time as a woman; all his subsequent lifetimes were male. He despised femaleness, femininity and weakness, yet he was effeminate.

So the only way he could get his female lifetimes included was to become an effeminate, gay man, where he took on the female role. Now this is not universal; only a small percentage of people that were gay came for regression and it is necessary to have hundreds of people to get an idea — but that was the case with him.

AMY: Of course, it makes perfect sense that the intellect would say, "Since women are routinely abused and victimized, I will not choose to be a woman again," although that soul was on a feminine wavelength.

SUE: That's right. Of course, in his prior lifetimes, he was like Attila the Hun, who treated his wife really badly, the same way that she was treated then. It has to do with getting too far out on the Mars end of things. His male lifetimes were very macho, in the army. I did find a consistency with homosexuality, that men being in a brotherhood of some sort, such as the army or navy or wherever there were no women, bred homosexuality.

AMY: Because the need for love never goes away - and for intimacy and sex ... so if you're confined in circumstances with your same sex, how can it be any other way?

SUE: This is why a young celibate priesthood isn't all that good. If you want to turn celibate when you're older or after you've had love and discovered what it was, that's one thing, but it's just asking for trouble to take a young man and to say, "You can't have sex." So the ministry is better when you can marry and you can have sex.

In other lifetimes, they really preferred men instead of women in this way. So often a warrior, which is what this man was... he was with Attila the Hun and the conquerors of the Roman legions, or whatever it was, fighting in the lands and having homosexual relationships, he was very macho. So, he comes in and he is very effeminate and very tied to his mother. He supposedly loved his mother, but he had rejected femininity.

AMY: Do you remember the outcome of your work with this homosexual?

SUE: Both of them responded to it tremendously; both were very moved by it and understood it. The thing that was amazing was that they seemed to understand things on a soul level in a way that their minds had never understood. It wasn't an intellectual thing; they profoundly understood something that made a difference. They never came back for any follow up work.

AMY: So, it seems the primary purpose of them incarnating, on a soul level, was to facilitate some peace between mother and son, and for her to accept him, as for him to accept himself, even though her conscious intention was to change him or help him to change.

SUE: Yes, but they understood why he was that way and that he might take a female lifetime the next time. He might be willing to because that was what he had to do.

AMY: Did the mother show up as a figure in his past lives, because it's often considered, you know, the stereotypical image of homosexuals as having the very dominant mother figure that they are rejecting by rejecting all women?

SUE: No, she wasn't. That theory never came up anywhere in my regression work with homosexuals. There was never that kind of a female in any of his lives. He sort of abandoned all the females and went with the men, but I think, because of the rejection of the female role, he became more closely identified in his own body and his own relationship with the mother. In other words, the mother was an ordinary mother and the boy goes into the service, discovers homosexuality, likes it, incarnates the next time and is in the service and discovers homosexuality. He's, meanwhile, marrying and having children, but by going into the service experiencing it, or into prison and experiencing it.

AMY: So, having the facade of a heterosexual, normal life, then?

SUE: Well, in those days, you didn't have to have too much of a facade. A man could do whatever he wanted to do.

AMY: So, it wasn't the same taboo as today.

SUE: He got married, had children, went to war, had homosexual experiences, came home, saw his wife, went to war and had more homosexual experiences. King Arthur and all his men probably did this too. But this macho-ness had gone to extremes and if you take any one thing and just want more of it — more and more military — you reach a point where you have to go to the opposite side. The pendulum will swing directly over to the feminine. So, he could no longer be Attila the Hun, gnashing his teeth. He was Mama's boy, and the closeness to the mother was probably to get the female energy. But I didn't find any causality of having a powerful mother that would make him homosexual. I think having the powerful mother was the result of rejecting feminine energy, wherein anything you repress and reject becomes stronger.

AMY: The polarity compelled him to be drawn back over and over again perhaps to a powerful mother because of the need to integrate the feminine.

SUE: You see, he would never stay with the women. From the time he was a child he's in military games and at fourteen years he goes into the army. He was very young when he would leave the women behind and doesn't have anything to do with femininity from that time. It was true also with the hunters and gatherers; the women would stay at home and the men would go off hunting for long periods of time in a group. Homosexuality was not thought of as being evil or wrong in many cultures.

AMY: Or perverse. There was no stigma attached.

SUE: Right. There was no religion in those tribal days.

AMY: So for them it was probably just a balanced lifestyle, that you had your family unit and also your adventures.

SUE: That's right. In the Greek and the Roman cultures, men were prized over women; if you had a male lover, he was more prized.

Anyway, in another case, this man came to me, and when I asked him his name, he said he had this secret, and if he told me his real name at birth, I could never tell anybody. The way he was talking made me wonder if he was a criminal hiding out, as he was new here. His soul record revealed that all of his lifetimes were very masculine and very violent. He was always dealing with conspiracies and plots and bombs and incendiary devices and wars. He related to the reading 100% and started telling me these totally unbelievable stories about strange people he had been involved with. He'd had no female lifetimes whatsoever. It wasn't until some time later that I realized that the name he had given me was a foreign name, so I didn't know it was a girl's name. He assumed that when he gave me the name and I would have known that it was a girl's name and that he was born a girl.

Later he confessed that he was born a girl. He'd had most of his sex change operation, but not all of it, and he was taking hormones and living as a man. He had moved here so that he could have a fresh start living as a man where nobody knew him as a woman or knew him at the intermediate stages of going from being a woman to being a man. When he was still a woman, he had lived as a lesbian, but he lost all of his lesbian lovers once he started to become a man, because they don't like men.

So, his intent was to marry a straight girl and maybe have some children, maybe she would have some children or they would adopt. But this was another case in which he had a very violent and very male, Martian energy.

Eventually he did marry a straight woman with children but the marriage didn't work out and he got a divorce. After that, he had crushes on other girls and they didn't work out.

One of the last things I remember was his being on my porch and saying, 'I should have stayed a woman; then at least I had love.' Because most straight women didn't want a man who didn't have all his equipment in place and couldn't have babies, and things like that, and gay women wouldn't touch him because he was too masculine looking.

He eventually moved away, to Santa Fe, when he felt that he had burned this area out somehow, although he had a strong support group here. He called me from Santa Fe and said that he was going to start a new life and counsel people like himself. They stopped doing the sex change operation, so he never got his sex change completed. They decided that people didn't benefit from it, so he was left half done.

Somehow, he fell in with some awful, weird people. He got scared of them and thought that they were going to assassinate him, so he bought a gun and at some point he was shot with that gun. People thought he committed suicide, but I wasn't sure if he did.

I held a memorial service for him in his favorite spot at Halibut Point. The service was amazing because his sister came from France, his stepmother came and all of these friends. Because he'd hated religion, all we did at this service was to share of our memories, so that we would support one another in our grieving. It was totally amazing how these people had kept his secret all the while. And when it came out that he was a transsexual, there were people at that service with their mouths hanging open, because they had never, ever guessed that he was a transsexual. But his stepmother shared that from the time that he/she was a little girl, she wanted to wear boy's clothes. I remember this poignant story about getting her ready for the first grade and taking her to the department story to buy little dresses. She went straight out of the little dress department, to the boys department to pick out boy's clothes.

So, from the time that he was little, he knew that he was a boy, and that's what he wanted to be. What he really wanted to be more than anything was a man married with children, and that's what he could never really have. He didn't want to be gay. He wanted to be a man and he really looked like a man.

AMY: It seems that the souls who are so tormented by the sex bodies that they have and the associated sex roles who go to the extreme of a sex change operation, must somehow feel a gross mistake was made and that they are correcting it. And that's where it's difficult to understand: did the spirit or the soul have a higher purpose in choosing that opposite sex body for this incarnation? How does one reconcile oneself spiritually?

SUE: The karma of desire. The way that we create our karma for ourselves is through desire and he always desired to be male. But the soul also has a higher purpose. You learn something from every lifetime, so that the soul extracts the wisdom from experience. I hope that he will sometime be able to take a female lifetime without cutting off his breasts.

AMY: These two cases seem to stand out because they are the exception to the rule, but that in more normal situations, you do find that individuals reincarnate as the opposite sex.

SUE: Yes, they stand out for that reason and they happen to be the first homosexual and the first transsexual who came to me.

AMY: In your more routine past life reviews, what impact does it have on people when they recognize that they were the opposite sex and that they are seeing the way they once were through their various relations with the opposite sex in this lifetime? Has there been a consistent pattern in terms of healing that takes place as a result of that?

SUE: Yes. People recognized what was being channeled about them so strongly in their choice of mates that they were attracted to, that realization was amazing. Sometimes they could change their patterns, once they had that realization, and no longer go after that type, or go after someone who was that type and reformed.

AMY: So, it's very empowering.

SUE: The most empowering thing people can do is to experience themselves as their opposite, because so much karma is created by being angry with your spouse or the men or the women in your life for being the way they are or for doing whatever they are doing. Because, you start to project everything out and you say, they're doing it to make me miserable.

AMY: Right, so they can abandon the victim or the martyr pattern. When they see that the soul chose that relationship out of a karmic necessity that they can now go beyond.

SUE: You know, it's not choice in the way we experience it. They don't have any choice in the matter because that's who they are, the male part of them is this way and the female part of them is that way, and that's what they attract. It's like a magnetic attraction. A magnet doesn't have any choice but to attract metal.

AMY: We used to say that you are what you eat. Well, it seems there's a parallel here: you are the person with whom you share a relationship, and we come to this understanding through this kind of work. And in doing that, the question of choice takes on a different perspective completely.

SUE: Often they could release the partner or might get a divorce. They could clear this pattern because something inside of them changed, which meant that what they attracted changed. The magnetism between souls changes when you transmute or release past blockages through understanding and forgiving. Of course, the highest understanding is that we are all part of one magnificent self, and that actually, every being that comes to us... our friends are the way we used to be as friends, our parents may be reflecting how we once were as parents, and so forth.

AMY: That's so powerful, that we are seeing ourselves as we once were. So, if we change our consciousness and no longer need that projection as a mirror to look at the past, it's as if we can choose a new social role-play in that relationship.

SUE: That's right. New spiritual energy enters so we can have and create new things. Deeply embedded psychic impressions from past lives are like knots that exist in the spiritual body and in the chakras and this repetitive karma happens for good or for bad. If something is wonderful, we want it to continue happening. If something is terrible, it gets imprinted so that it becomes repetitive.

By repeating addictive behaviors, you know, we've gone off, we cheated on the little woman, we gambled, we did anything we wanted to do, we didn't support the kids, and we did it over and over again that whole lifetime, and then the next lifetime and then the next — Bang! Eventually we get the lifetime where we're sitting at home wondering where he is while he's out gambling and womanizing and not supporting the kids.

AMY: So, a refusal to grow beyond a pattern necessitates that you find yourself on a receiving end of that indiscretion.

SUE: That's right. You're stuck in a deeply embedded unconscious impression, doing these over and over again. And often, you're exactly the opposite. So you become the very upright woman who is dutiful, home taking care of the children, and doing all the right things. Because that's what you refused to be, this upright and dutiful and staying-at-home and taking-care-of-the-stuff — you become the polarity you rejected.

It's the same way with money and power. The people who were very powerful, who were kings and queens and who ruled over other people, had to become the lowest. That was their polarity. They became absolutely the lowest rungs, whether it's a leper or some other lowly person in society. There are many stories of kings and of high beings who became lepers – or some other person in society. The people who'd had all this money, especially if they didn't do any good and were selfish with it, had to become penniless. But, then, in the case of someone who gave to charities and helped the sick, and so forth, they may not have had much money, but they would always be helped when they were sick. So, that came back to them. So, everything we give out comes back to us in some way.

AMY: The point is the same; the soul yearns to achieve empathy, so that if in a position of power you have no empathy for those without it, you must come back as the opposite in order to understand that experience. It's the same with the Dual-Gender Soul concept; we must have empathy for our opposite-sex as much as for ourselves.

SUE: Well, the guru, of course, the enlightened being, feels everything that everybody else feels and sees everything. So, when you talk of God, God is not somewhere outside of us, but is inside of us, seeing through our eyes, hearing through our ears and God feels everything that goes on within the body.

When empathy is the rule, every living thing lives in harmony. As such, if I were to do something that hurts you, I would feel it, so why would I do anything to hurt you? If people open their souls and love each other, we would see that we are really only one being.

AMY: Fascinating. It's like the mind became God instead of being in the mind of God.

SUE: What the Guru does is dissolve the ego so that you experience your oneness with everything and everyone in the universe, so that you can no longer be a harmful person. Because if you were to harm someone it would harm you probably more than the person today, because people have hard ego shells around them and you can insult them and they'll sometimes laugh. But, if you were totally open and empathetic, you wouldn't be able to laugh. So, in this way, you gather together all the aspects of your consciousness. You no longer split off from the aspects of your consciousness that manifest as your husband or wife, as your mother or father, your children, as your friends, as the people you encounter in the streets, etc. So, it's difficult for people to understand because of the fact that it sounds like blaming the victim. This is why this knowledge really wasn't given out to people, because they couldn't understand it, and because their emotional nature is such that they would become totally absorbed in feeling sorry for this person, on this person's side or that person's side.

At the end of every age, the records are opened. We read about it in the Bible when they talk about the Book of Life. That's what the records are, each person's Book of Life. It's great when a person can have their records opened and transmute these things, because the negatives go on, reoccurring over and over again.

AMY: Thank you so much. Sue! This has been wonderful!

SUE: You're so welcome!

"The Bride's Debt"
Contributed by Rabbi Yonassan Gershom

Rabbi Gershom's newest book, Jewish Reincarnation Stories, contains the following tale from the classical sixteenth-century Hebrew text, Shivchei Ha-Ari. This story is wonderfully apropos of much has been discussed relative to Dual-Gender Souls and the laws of karma and grace. Rabbi Gershom was both generous and thoughtful in suggesting that it be included in this book and for his additional comments, which following the story:

The Holy Ari ("Lion" in Hebrew) was Rabbi Isaac Luria, who is still regarded as a great master of kabbalah [system of interpretation of the Scriptures developed in the Middle Ages by certain rabbis], in Jewish history. That Rabbi Luria believed in and taught reincarnation is well known among scholars of Jewish mysticism. In addition to being able to read past lives, he also prescribed the appropriate tikkun (spiritual remedy) necessary for each individual soul's healing. In the context of Orthodox Judaism, Rabbi Luria was not unlike to a modern past-life therapist.

It happened in Safed that a disciple of the Holy Ari had to go on a long journey. Before departing, he came to his teacher for a letter of recommendation. The Ari wrote it for him then blessed him and said, "May God be with you, and may you go in peace."

The disciple then asked, "Master, can you tell me anything about what will happen when I get there?"

The Ari replied, "You will marry a beautiful woman and she is your destined soul mate for this life. But after you have been happily married for only six months, she will suddenly die. The reason is that in another incarnation, this woman was a man and you were also a man then. He was your dearest friend but he also caused you some legal trouble for six months. He finally brought a lawsuit against you in the civil courts, which caused you to lose 600 gold coins, even though you were innocent of his charges.

The Ari continued, "Now, this friend from another life is once again reincarnated, this time as the woman you will marry on your journey. His soul has come to make atonement for his sins against you. For six months of trouble that he caused in that life, you will have six months of happiness in this life. The inheritance you will receive when she dies is to repay you for the 600 gold pieces you lost in the past life. But even though you now know this, you should be kind and patient to this woman, and grant her forgiveness for the trouble she caused you in your previous lives."

And everything happened exactly as the Holy Ari said it would.

Many of the stories about Rabbi Luria address questions from his disciples about "redemption of the soul" or what is called "karma" in today's terminology. In the case of "The Bride's Debt," the rabbi not only foretold and explained the bride's future death, but also gave the prospective husband a context for understanding why his beloved would be taken from him so suddenly. The disciple accepted this explanation and was then advised to treat his wife with understanding even though he now knew she was the soul who wronged him in a past life.

IN CLOSING: THE DUAL-GENDER LEGACY

For many of the dual-gender souls whose stories were presented, synchronistic events in a therapeutic setting brought healing and spiritual transformation. Beyond these dozens of stories substantiating the theory of dual-gender souls, we journeyed the paths of souls who reincarnated in different cultures, classes, races and religions. As such, when we reclaim our past lives, we also broaden our "familiarity" with all of humanity, affirming that, in the truest sense, we are all brothers and sisters. The developmental road that led to the idea of dual-gender souls was paved decades ago through the courageous, pioneering work of psychologist Carl Jung. Jung's theory of anima and animus recognized that our unconscious minds contain qualities assigned to the opposite sex. By consciously retrieving this hidden opposite-sexuality, such as through past life regression, a true emancipation can occur that balances the *yin* and *yang* aspects of our nature.

Awareness of our dual-gender natures fosters empathy and understanding in male-female relations. Freed from the trap of attaching gender identity to the biological sex, the dual-gender soul can fulfill his/her potential, regardless of popular culture shifts that reconstruct social norms based upon biological equipment. To dwell in dual-gender soul awareness is to have a consciousness of equity, where male and female polarities are synthesized in the psyche. As such, we evolve toward a wholeness of being that may be the greatest achievement to which we can aspire, generating an immeasurable wealth of healing and inner peace. Men and women need each other in order to become balanced for worldly purposes and to gain understanding of our inner-opposite-genders.

The legacy of our dual-gender souls is to transcend psychosocial stereotypes and prejudices so that we can live more lovingly, with compassion, where women freely celebrate and manifest their creative drives, and men appreciate and cherish their receptive natures.

RESOURCES

While many authors on the subject of reincarnation have been sources of inspiration, two visionaries most guided my path and are mentioned in this text: Isabel Hickey and William Swygard. Both have passed onto the other side:

Hickey, Isabel, It Is All Right. 1976.

Swygard, William, Awareness Techniques. 1971. (The Multi-Plane Awareness Techniques Instructions can be found at http://whirlitzer.org/swygard.html)

Made in the
USA
Middletown, DE